# New York Mosaic Color by Number Coloring Book for Adults

## By Color Questopia

# Thank you
# for your purchase!

## Claim your FREE digital copy of our
## Highlight Reel Color By Number Book:

## Check out our website: colorquestopia.com

## Join our Facebook group:
## facebook.com/colorquestopia

## Follow us on Instagram: @colorquestopia

## Did you enjoy this book?
## Please leave us a review!

## https://geni.us/cqreview

# Color By Number Tips

1. **Relax and have fun**
   Let your cares slip away as you color the images. Take your time. Coloring is a meditative activity and there's no wrong way to do it. Feel free to color as you listen to music, watch TV, lounge in bed- do whatever relaxes you most! You can also color while you're out and about- on the train or at a cafe- take the book with you anywhere you go. Coloring is therapeutic and is great for stress relief and relaxation!

2. **Colors corresponding to each number are shown on the back cover of the book**
   Each number corresponds to a color shown on the back of the book. You can match the color as closely as you like- but feel free to change the color or the shade if you don't have the exact color match- that's totally fine. Although this is a color by number book, it's completely okay to get creative and color the images with whichever colors you like and have. The numbers are there to be a guide and to allow you to color without having to focus your energy on choosing colors.

3. **Choose your coloring tools**
   Everyone has their favorite coloring markers, crayons, pencils, pens- even paints! Feel free to color with any tool that you like! If you choose markers or paints, we recommend putting a blank sheet of paper or cardboard behind each image, so that your colors don't run onto the next image.

   Enjoy!

1. Yellow

2. Dark Brown

3. Light Yellow

4. Brown

5. Dark Red

6. Medium Brown

7. Violet

8. Light Brown

9. Light Red

10. Orange

11. Pink

12. Light Orange

13. Green

14. Light Green

15. Dark Gray

16. Gray

17. Light Gray

18. Red

19. Sky Blue

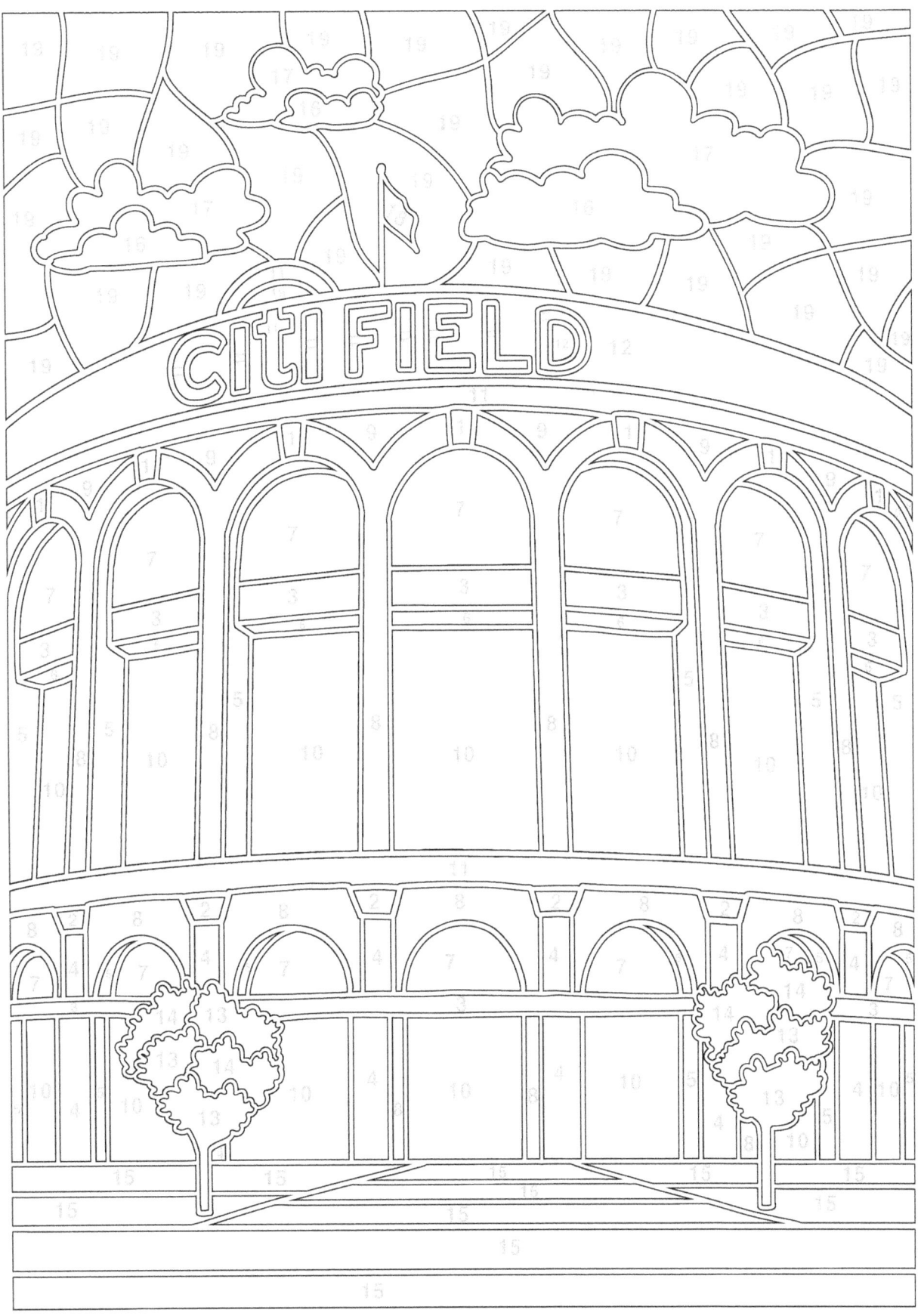

1. Red

2. Brown

3. Orange

4. Medium Brown

5. Dark Red

6. Dark Brown

7. Light Violet

8. Gray

9. Light Red

10. Light Orange

11. Light Purple

12. Purple

13. Violet

14. Light Gray

15. Blue

16. Navy Blue

17. Sky Blue

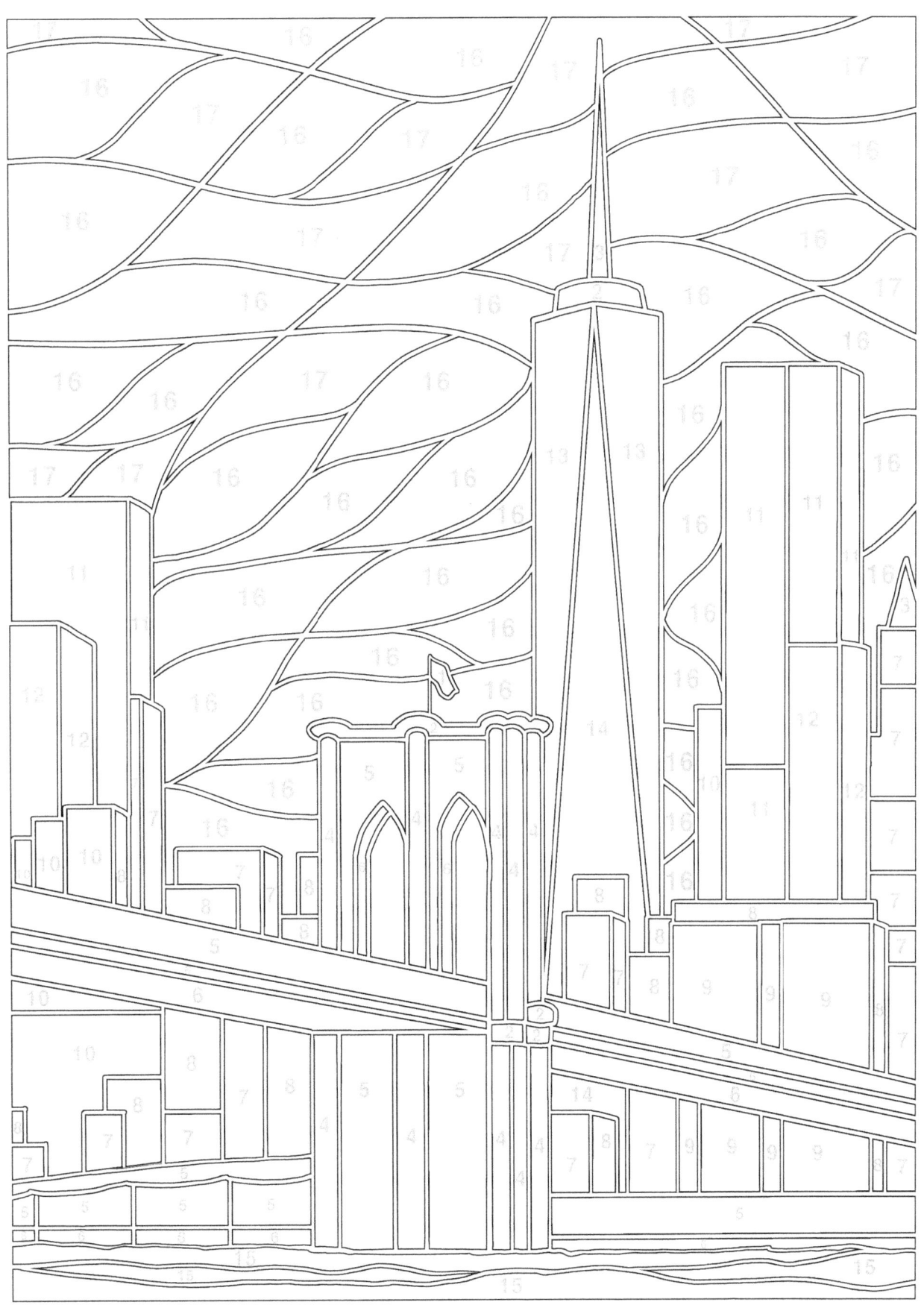

1. Orange

2. Yellow

3. Light Yellow

4. Dark Red

5. Brown

6. Sky Blue

7. Blue

8. Light Pink

9. Light Orange

10. Red

11. Dark Brown

12. Dark Orange

13. Dark Gray

14. Light Gray

15. Light Violet

16. Violet

17. Light Purple

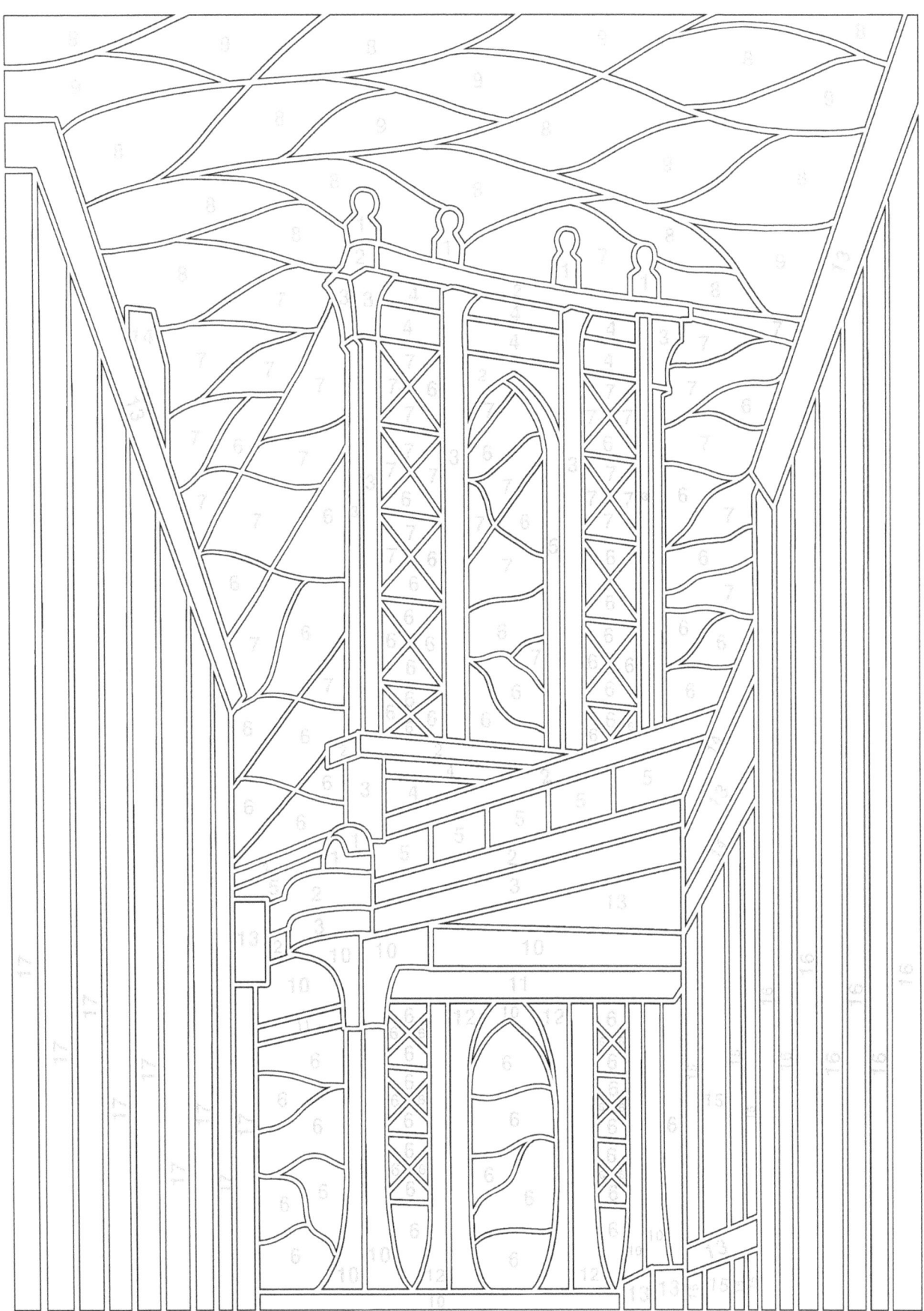

1. Yellow

2. Dark Yellow

3. Light Violet

4. Light Orange

5. Red

6. Dark Red

7. Dark Brown

8. Light Brown

9. Light Red

10. Dark Gray

11. Gray

12. Medium Brown

13. Navy Blue

14. Medium Yellow

15. Dark Orange

16. Brown

17. Sky Blue

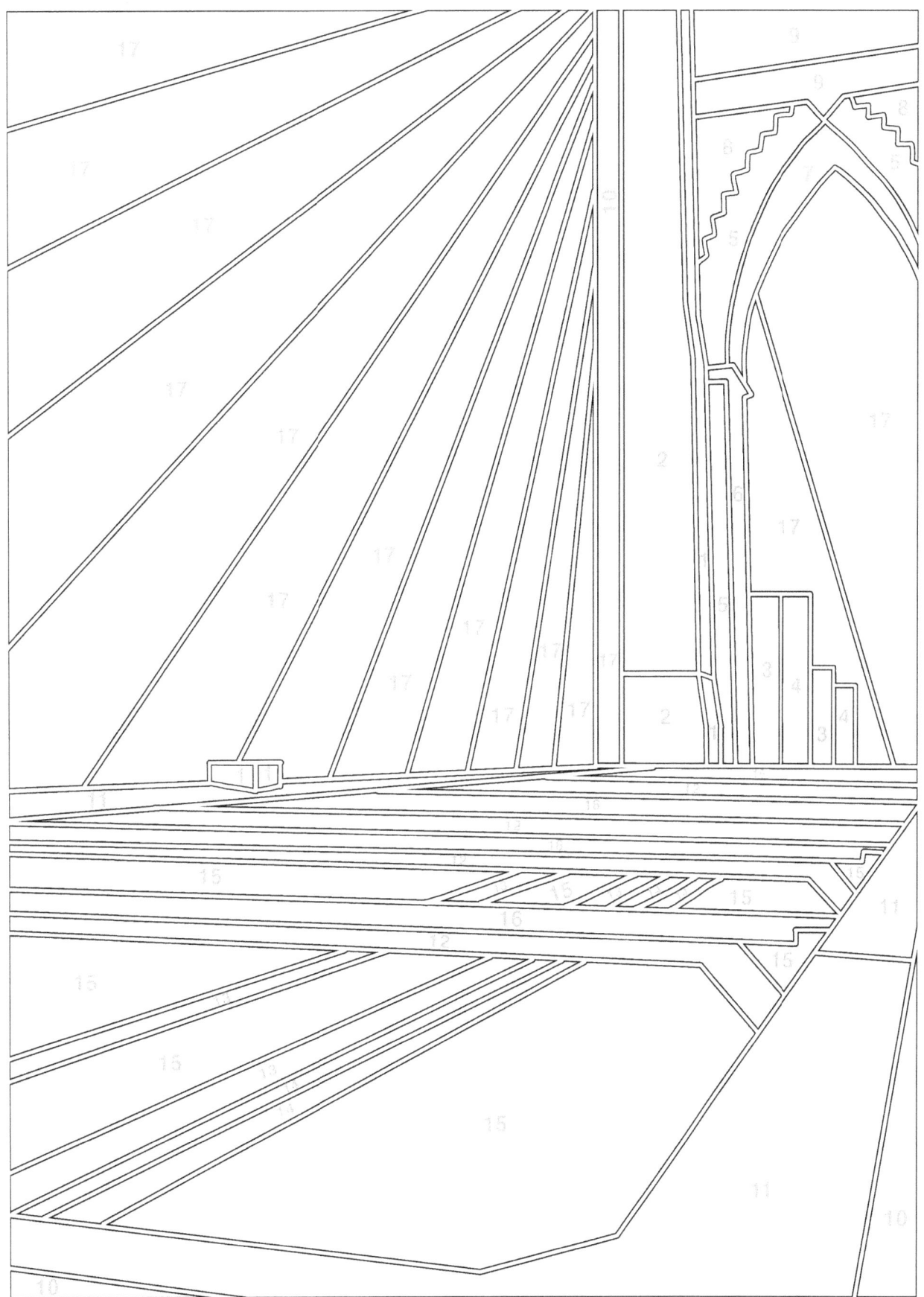

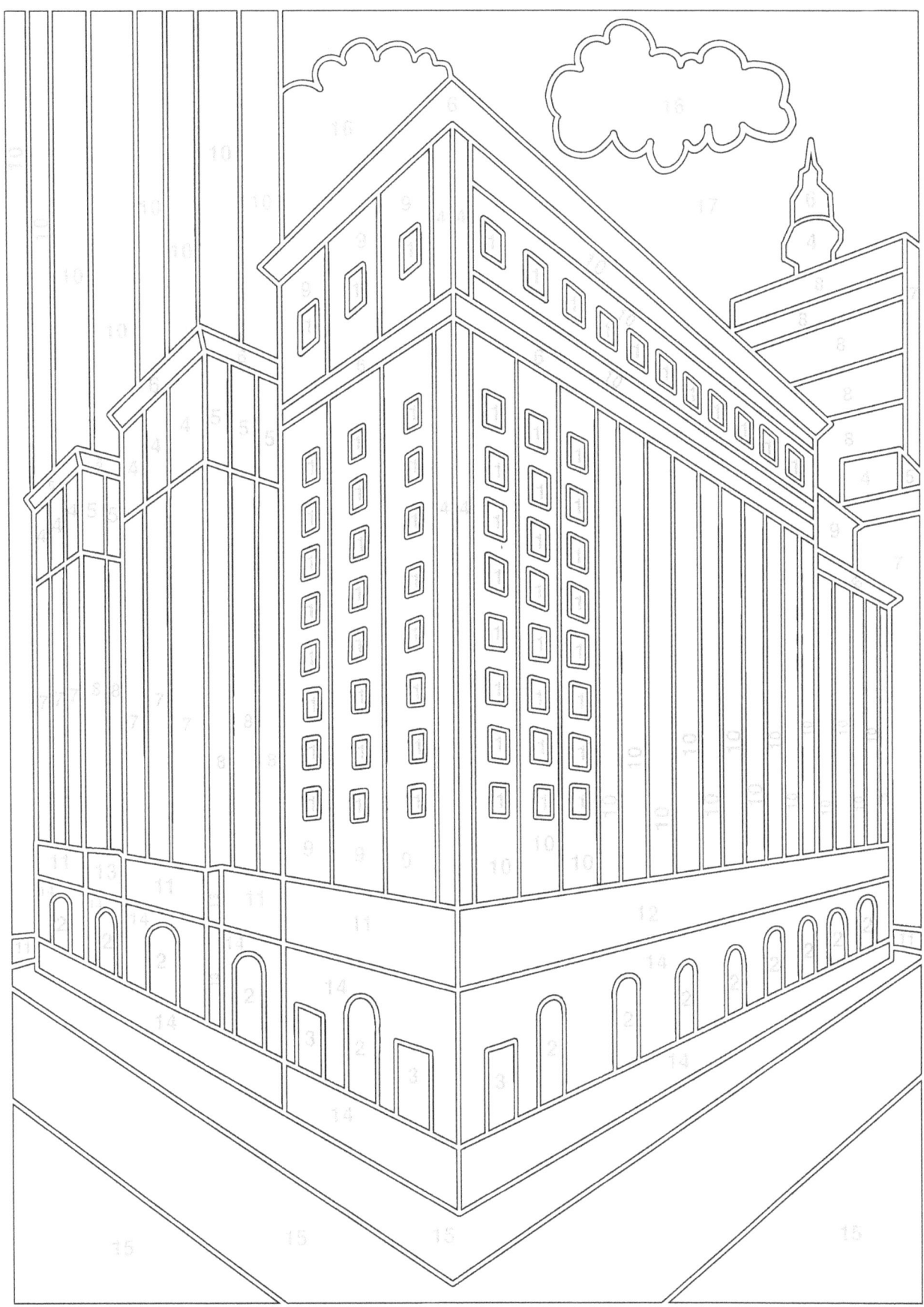

1. Orange

2. Dark Brown

3. Brown

4. Violet

5. Dark Red

6. Medium Brown

7. Dark Orange

8. Light Brown

9. Light Red

10. Dark Gray

11. Gray

12. Light Gray

13. Medium Blue

14. Light Blue

15. Light Pink

16. Light Orange

17. Light Yellow

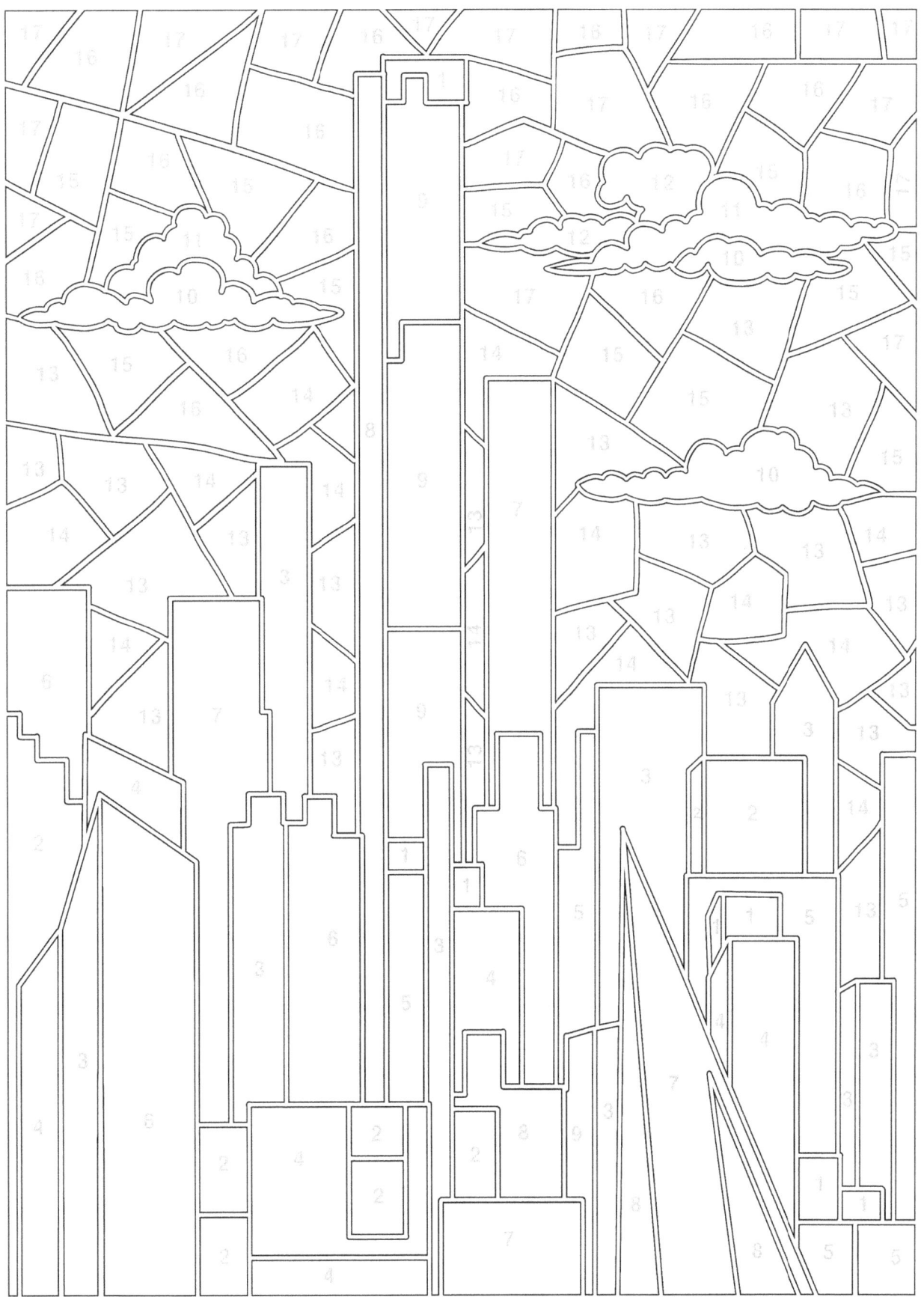

1. Orange

2. Dark Brown

3. Pink

4. Yellow

5. Dark Red

6. Medium Brown

7. Red

8. Light Brown

9. Light Red

10. Light Orange

11. Light Pink

12. Violet

13. Light Violet

14. Light Blue

15. Blue

16. Gray

17. Light Gray

18. Sky Blue

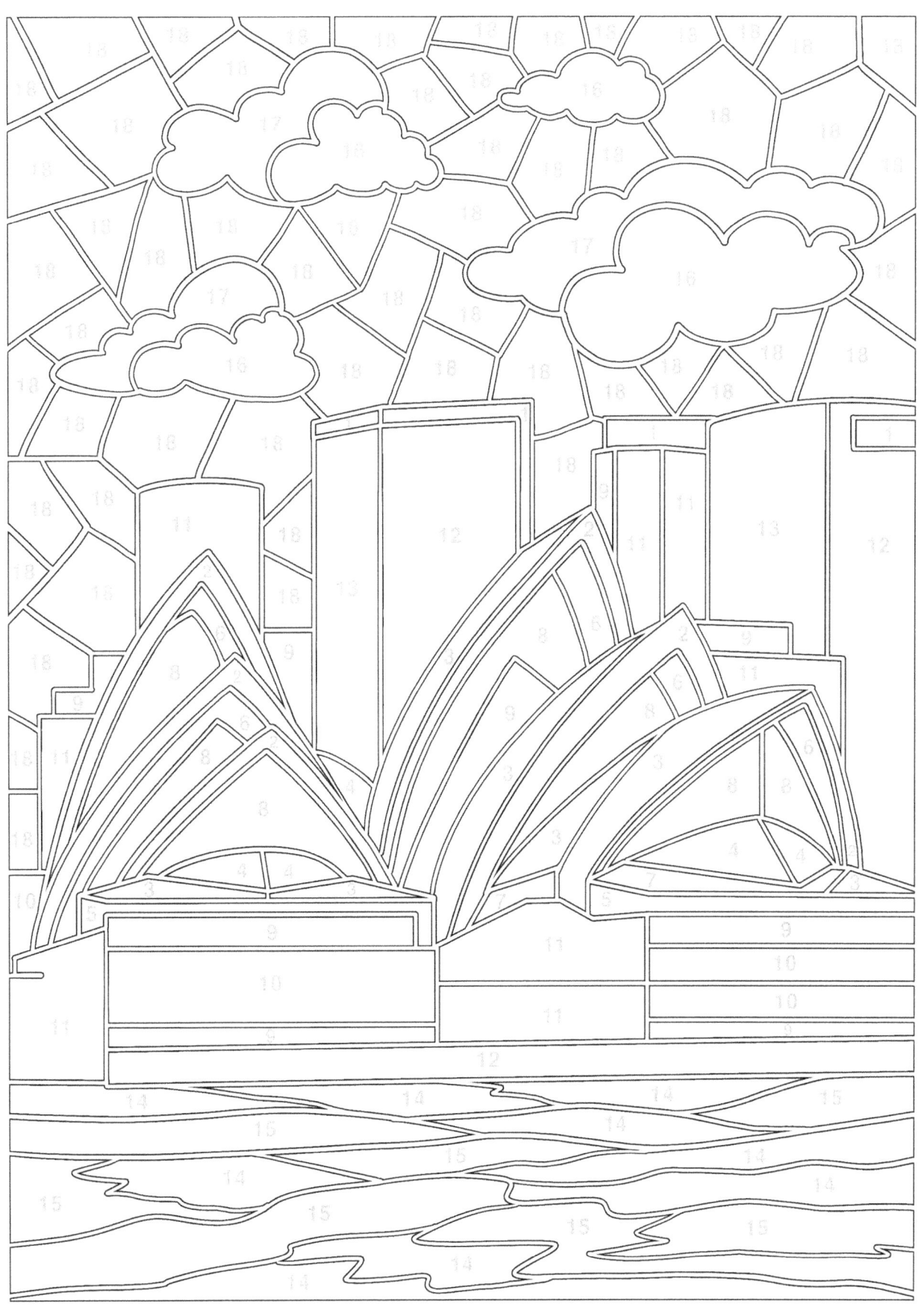

1. Yellow
2. Light Yellow
3. Brown
4. Medium Brown
5. Light Brown
6. Light Orange
7. Violet
8. Dark Violet
9. Red
10. Dark Gray
11. Light Gray
12. Gray
13. Medium Gray
14. Gray Purple
15. Dark Brown
16. White
17. Sky Blue

1. Red
2. Light Orange
3. Brown
4. Yellow
5. Light Red
6. Medium Brown
7. Pink
8. Light Purple
9. Dark Orange
10. Orange
11. Light Brown
12. Dark Brown
13. Dark Violet
14. Violet
15. Light Gray
16. Blue
17. Light Blue

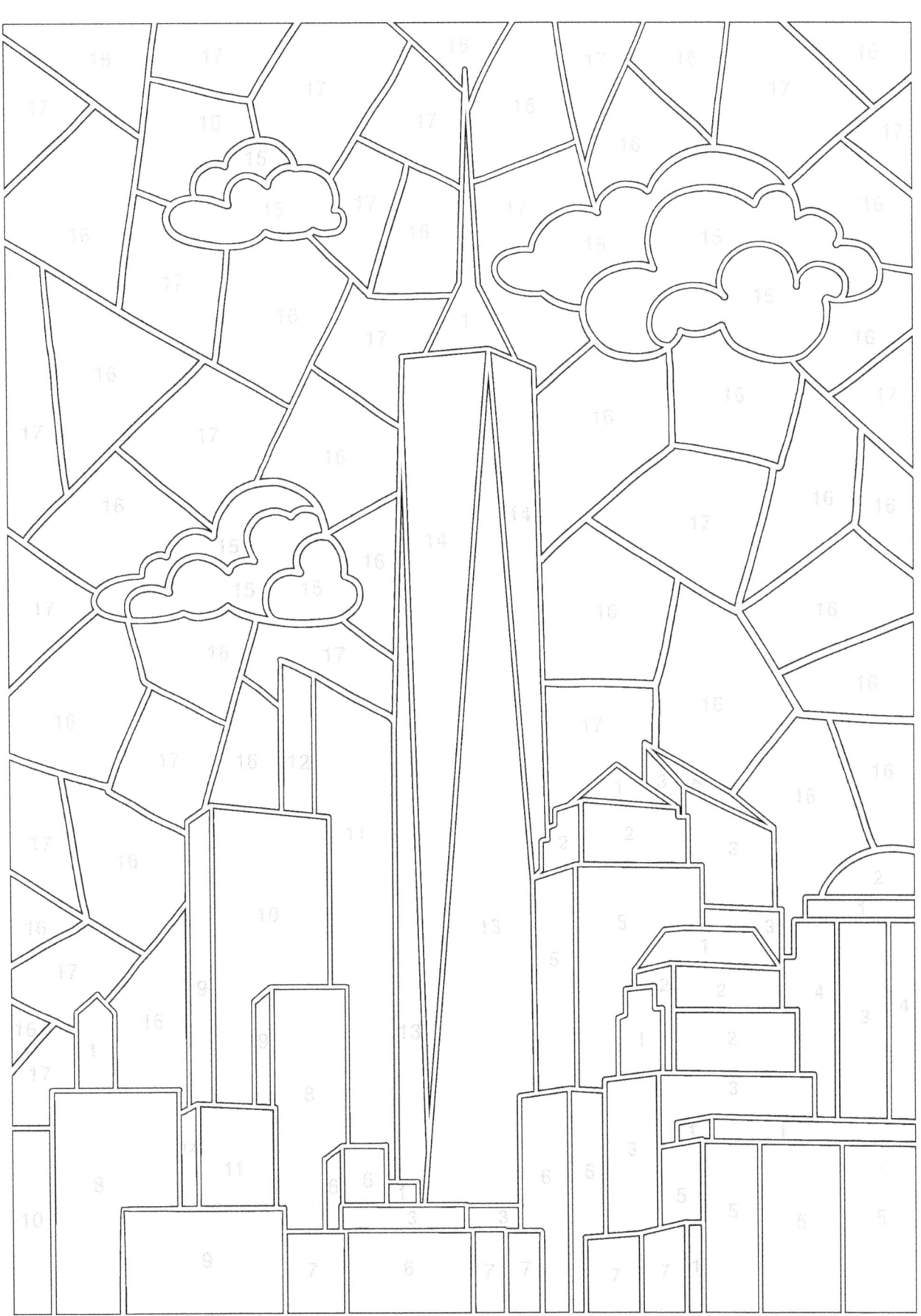

1. Yellow

2. Dark Brown

3. Brown

4. Light Violet

5. Dark Red

6. Light Red

7. Dark Violet

8. Orange

9. Dark Orange

10. Light Brown

11. Pink

12. Medium Orange

13. Light Yellow

14. Dark Gray

15. White

16. Blue

17. Light Blue

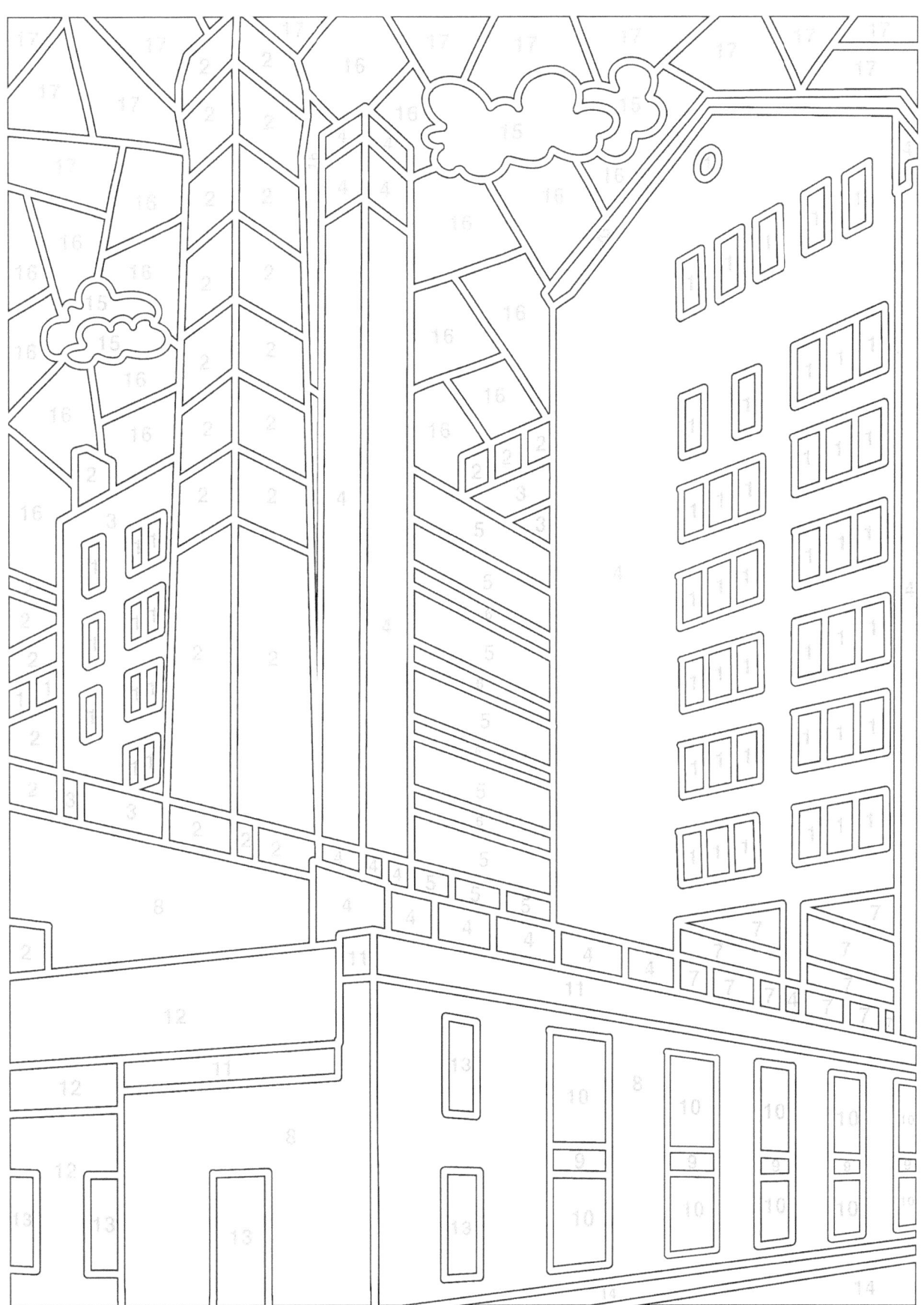

1. Yellow

2. Dark Orange

3. Light Gray

4. Light Brown

5. Light Orange

6. Gray

7. Dark Gray

8. Brown

9. Dark Brown

10. Violet

11. Dark Violet

12. Orange

13. Light Blue

14. Dark Blue

15. White

16. Medium Blue

17. Sky Blue

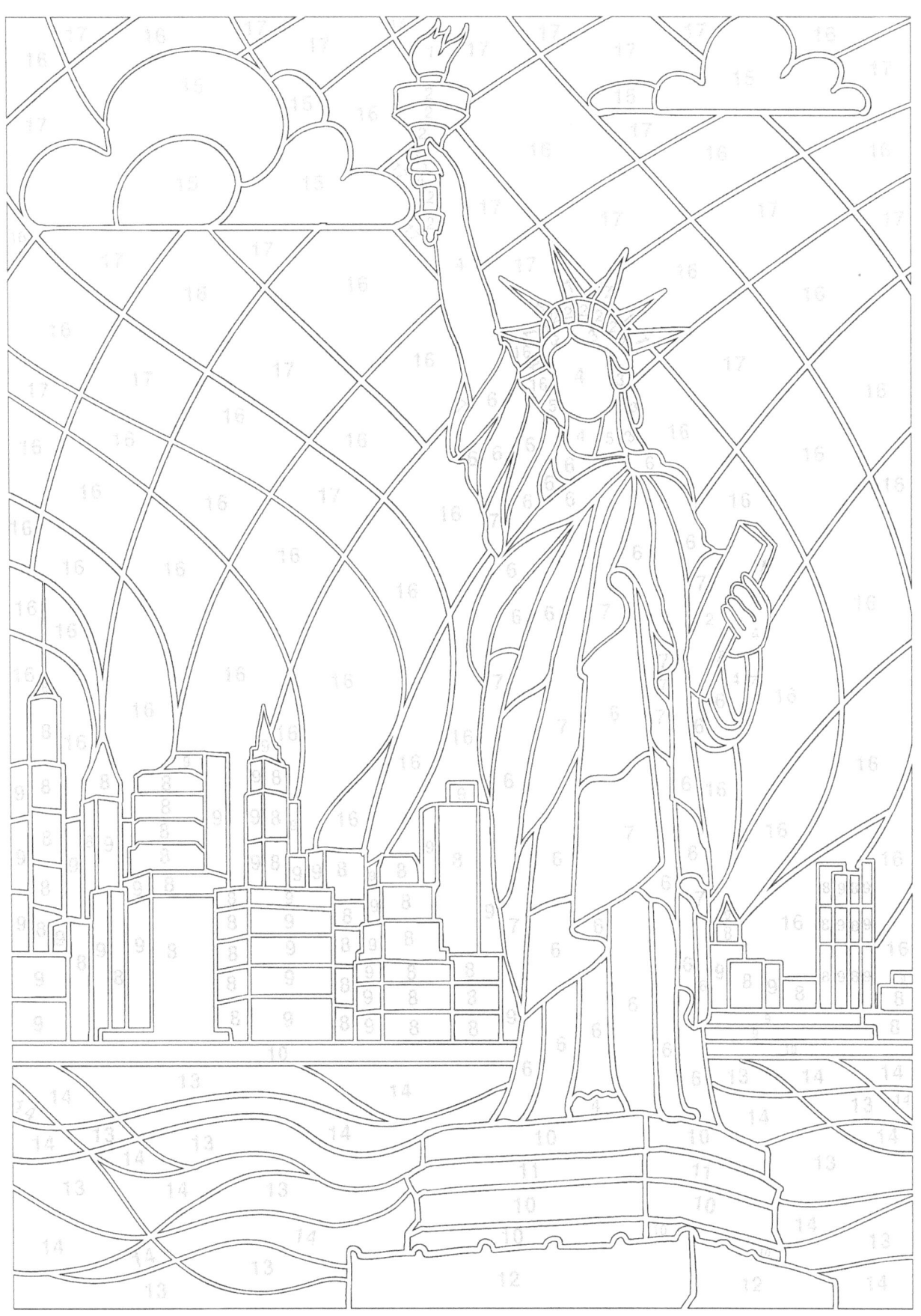

1. Yellow

2. Dark Orange

3. Light Orange

4. Red

5. Medium Brown

6. Dark Red

7. Light Brown

8. Light Yellow

9. Light Red

10. Dark Gray

11. Dark Brown

12. Brown

13. Orange

14. Gray

15. Light Gray

16. Blue

17. Sky Blue

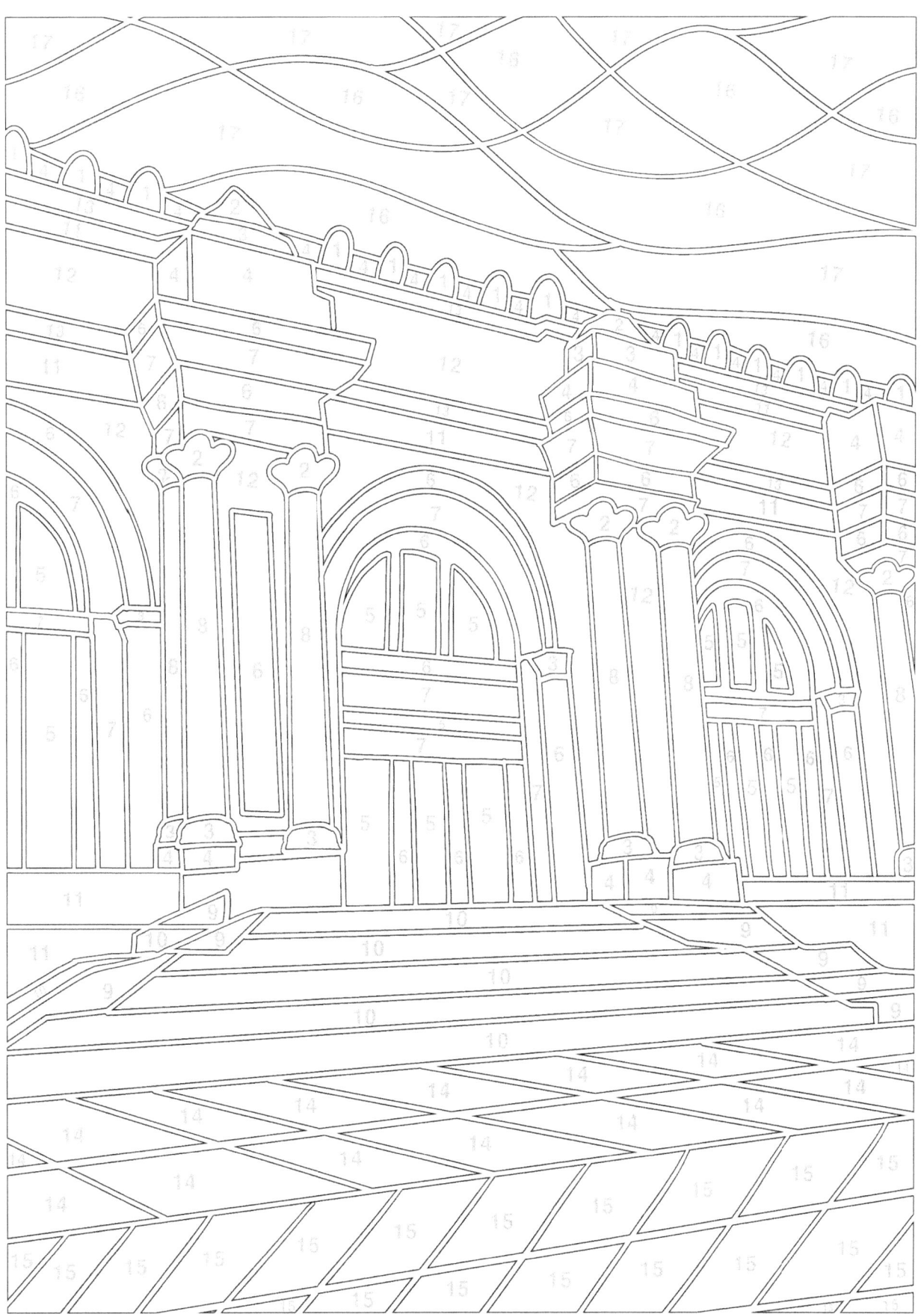

1. Red

2. Yellow

3. Pink

4. Light Red

5. Orange

6. Light Orange

7. Medium Brown

8. Light Brown

9. Brown

10. Medium Orange

11. Dark Orange

12. Dark Blue

13. Light Blue

14. Gray

15. Light Gray

16. Medium Blue

17. Sky Blue

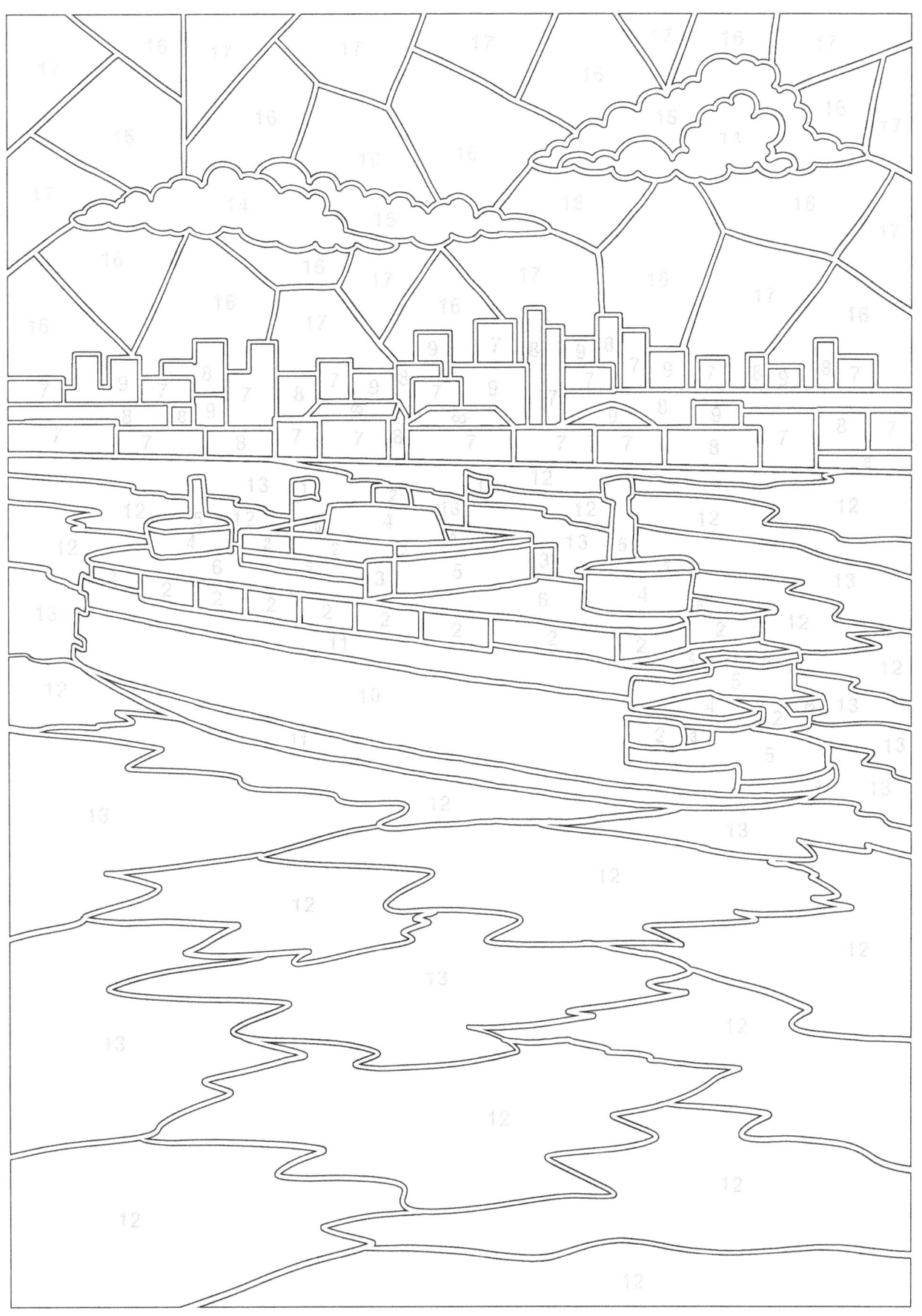

1. Red

2. Orange

3. Light Yellow

4. Brown

5. Medium Brown

6. Dark Brown

7. Light Brown

8. Light Orange

9. Light Red

10. Dark Orange

11. Medium Orange

12. Green

13. Light Green

14. Gray

15. Light Gray

16. Blue

17. Light Blue

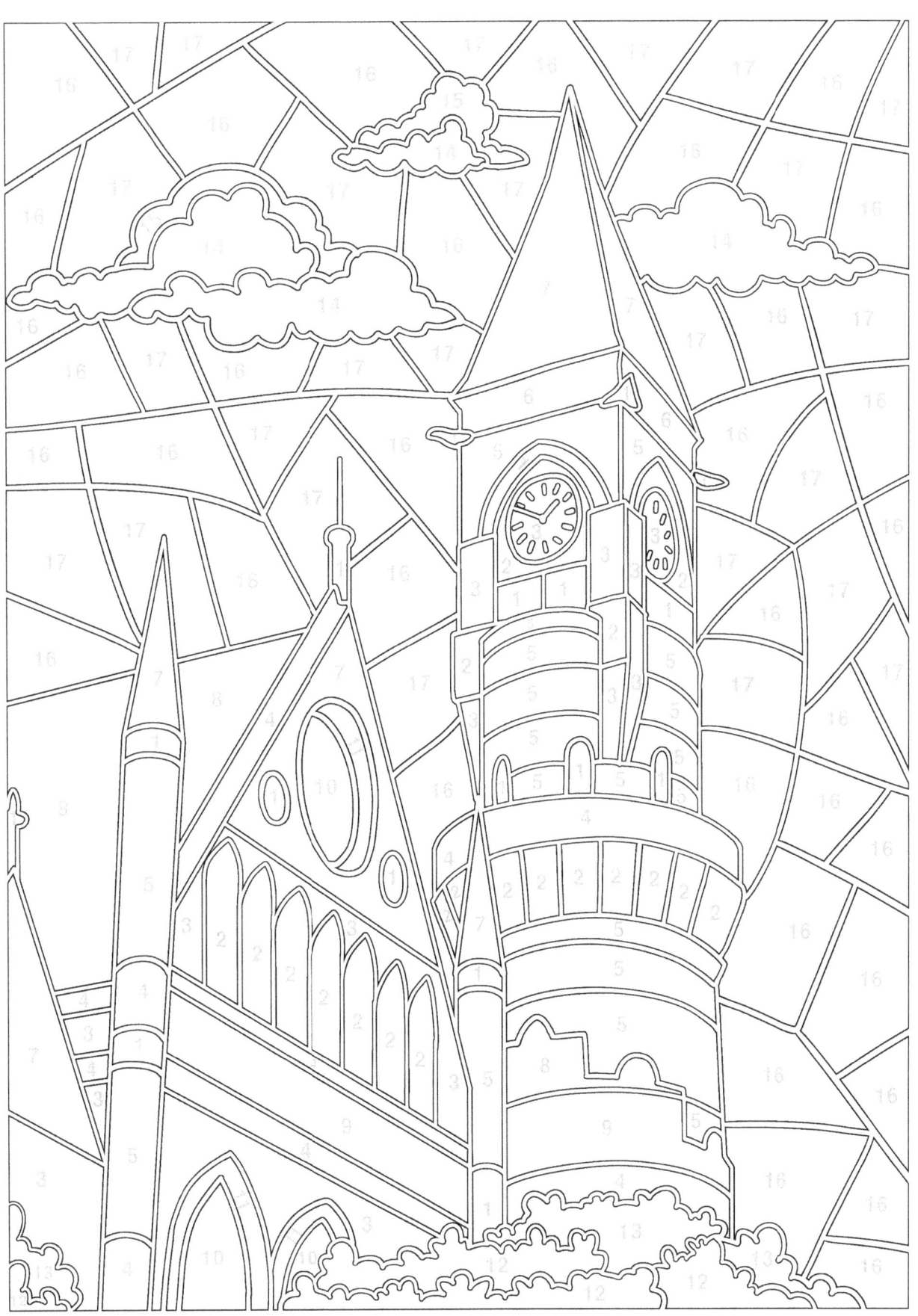

1. Yellow

2. Dark Brown

3. Light Yellow

4. Brown

5. Dark Red

6. Light Brown

7. Light Pink

8. Pink

9. Dark Pink

10. Orange

11. Dark Orange

12. Dark Gray

13. Light Green

14. Blue

15. Sky Blue

16. Gray

17. Light Gray

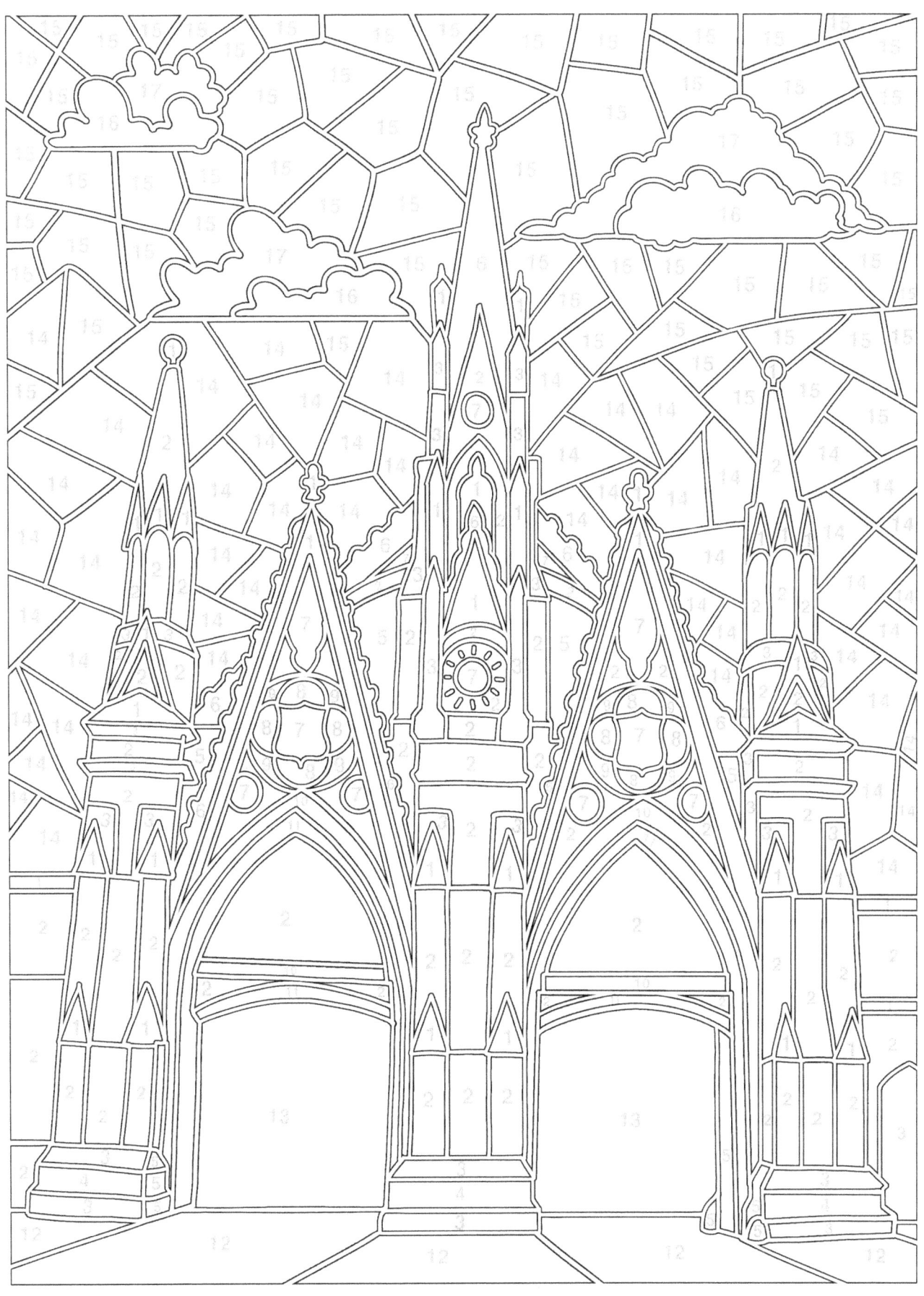

1. Yellow

2. Light Yellow

3. Dark Orange

4. Orange

5. Light Brown

6. Brown

7. Dark Brown

8. Light Red

9. Red

10. Violet

11. Light Violet

12. Light Orange

13. Dark Gray

14. Gray

15. Light Gray

16. Blue

17. Sky Blue

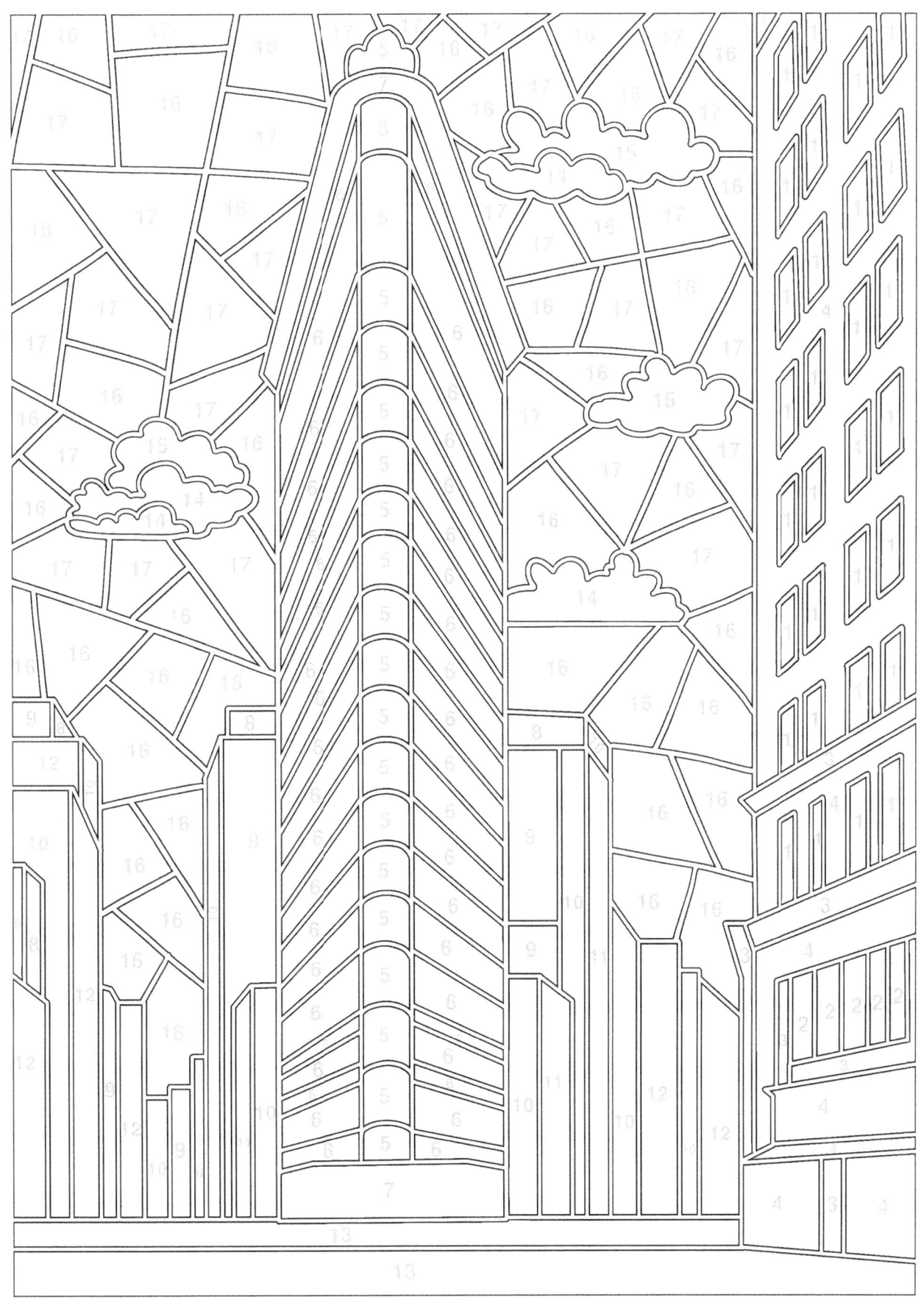

1. Yellow
2. Light Yellow
3. Brown
4. Light Pink
5. Dark Orange
6. Pink
7. Orange
8. Violet
9. Light Brown
10. Dark Violet
11. Medium Violet
12. Dark Brown
13. Dark Blue
14. Light Blue
15. Blue
16. Sky Blue
17. Gray
18. Light Gray

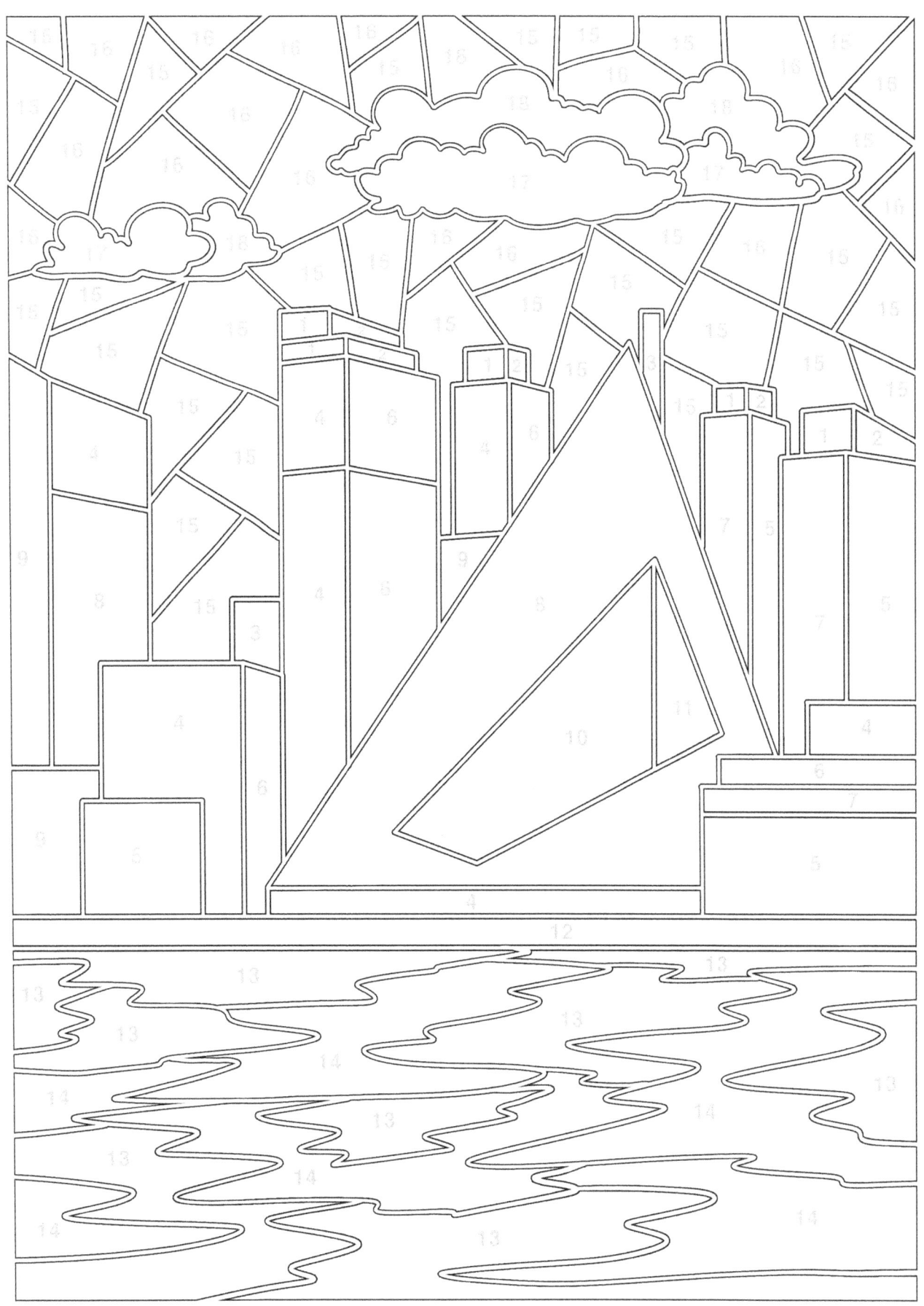

1. Brown

2. Yellow

3. Dark Brown

4. Medium Brown

5. Dark Red

6. Light Red

7. Gray

8. Dark Gray

9. Light Orange

10. Orange

11. Dark Orange

12. Light Gray

13. Blue

14. Light Blue

15. Dark Violet

16. Violet

17. Light Violet

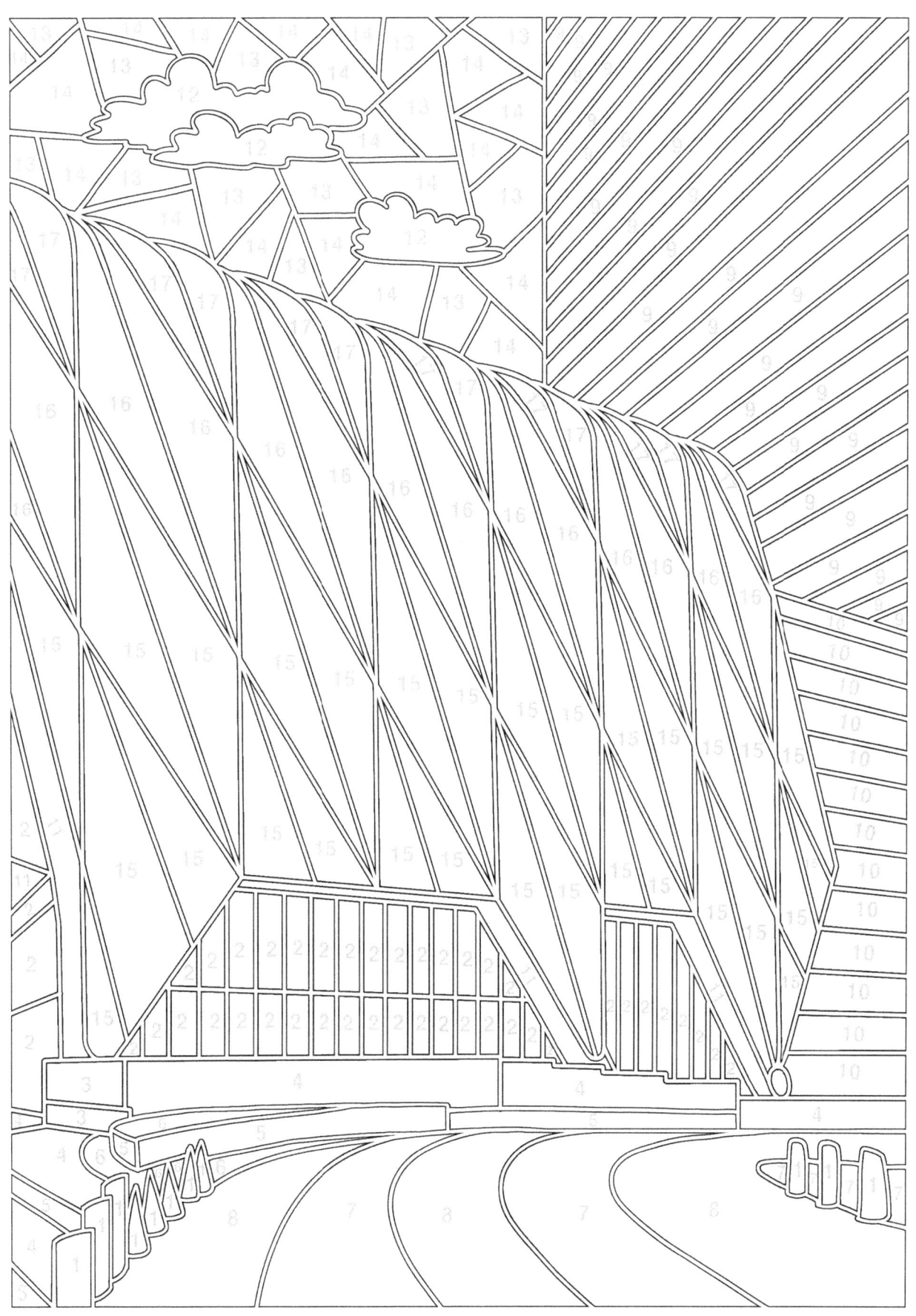

1. Orange
2. Yellow
3. Light Yellow
4. Pink
5. Dark Red
6. Medium Brown
7. Light Orange
8. Dark Brown
9. Light Red
10. Red
11. Brown
12. Gray
13. Light Gray
14. Dark Gray
15. Blue
16. Medium Blue
17. Sky Blue

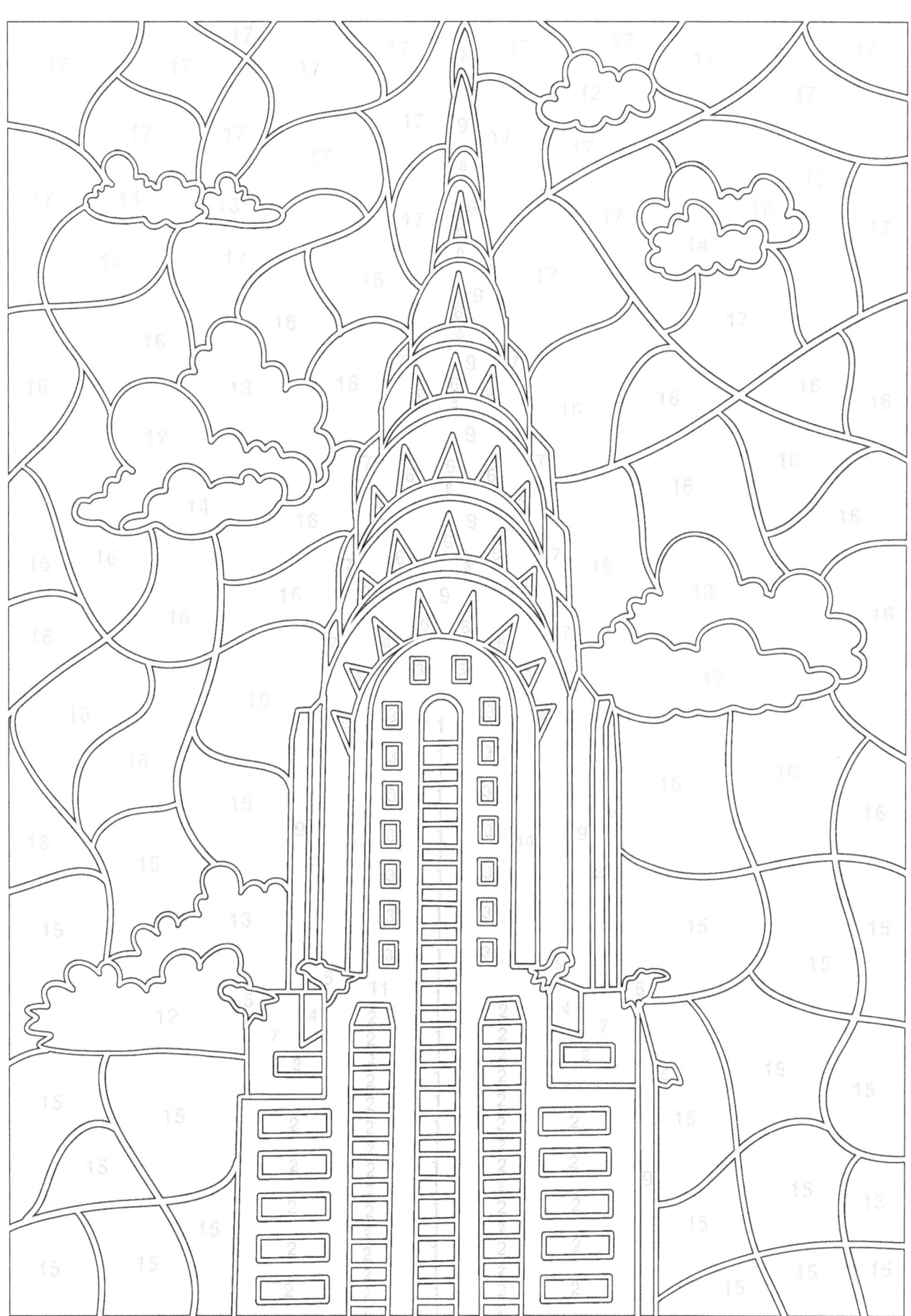

1. Light Violet

2. Light Red

3. Light Yellow

4. Red

5. Dark Red

6. Medium Brown

7. Light Brown

8. Brown

9. Dark Orange

10. Orange

11. Dark Green

12. Light Green

13. Green

14. Dark Gray

15. Dark Blue

16. Blue

17. Gray

18. Light Gray

19. Sky Blue

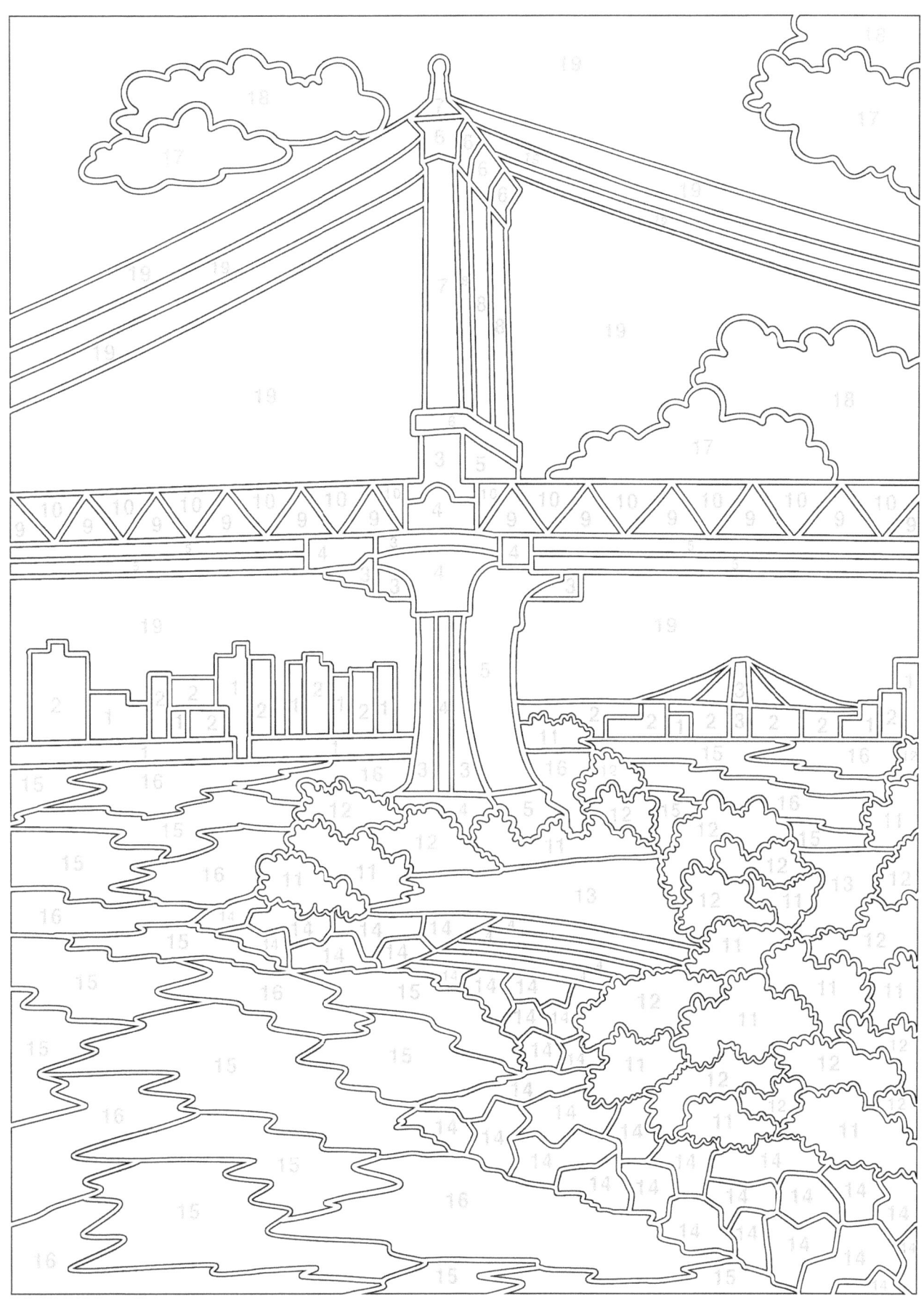

# ENJOY BONUS IMAGES FROM SOME OF OUR OTHER FUN COLOR BY NUMBER BOOKS!

# FIND ALL OF OUR BOOKS ON AMAZON

Easy Design
Adult Color By Number
Jumbo Coloring Book of Large Print
Flowers, Birds, and Butterflies

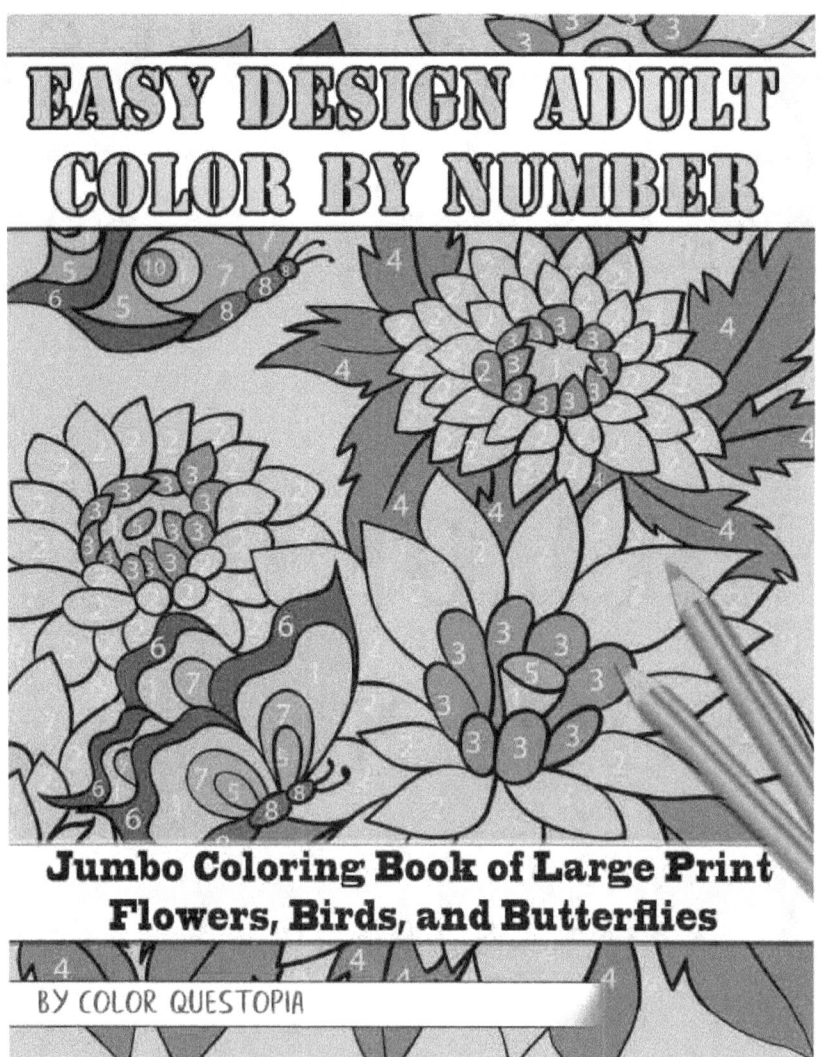

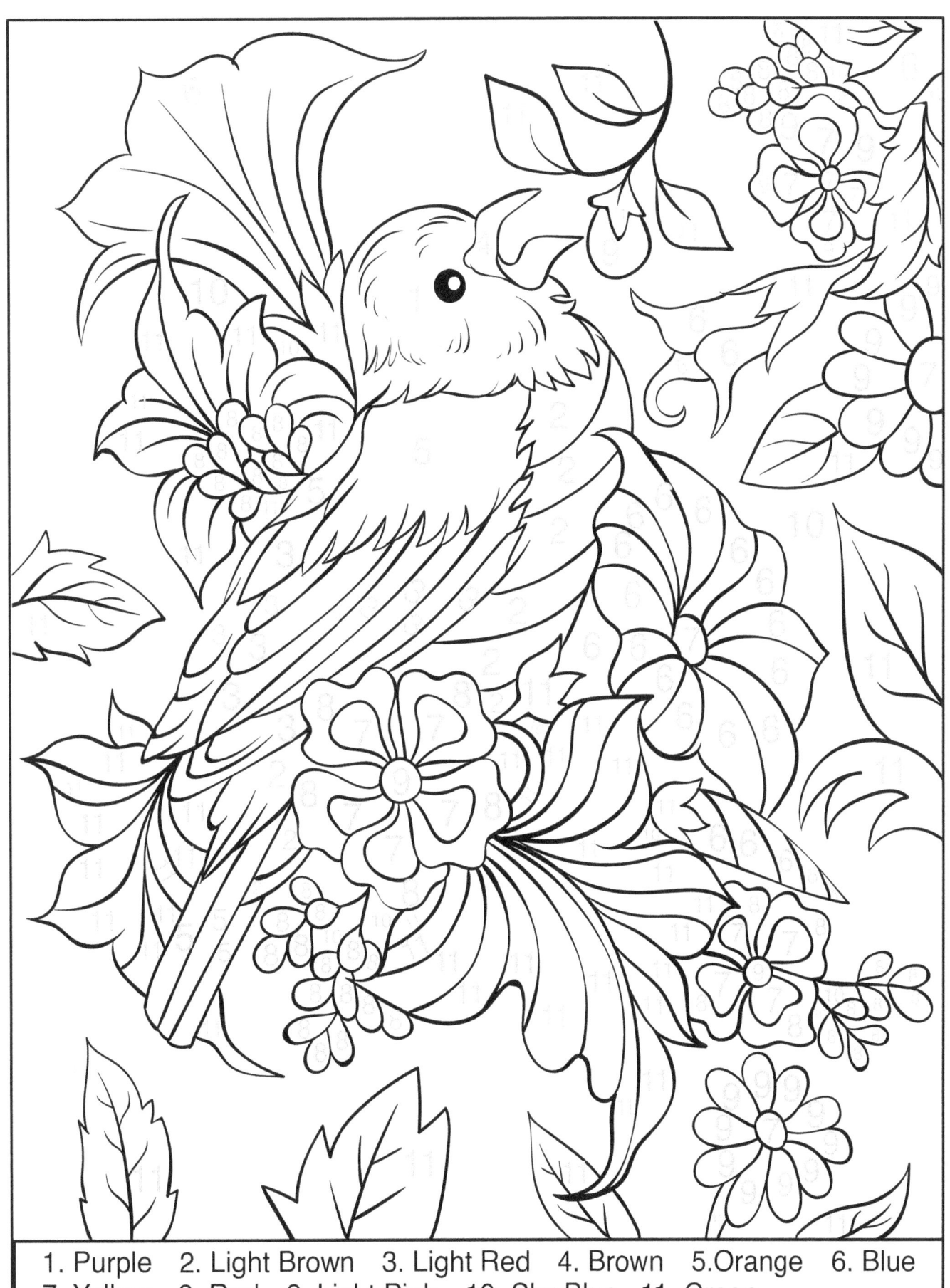

1. Purple   2. Light Brown   3. Light Red   4. Brown   5.Orange   6. Blue
7. Yellow   8. Red   9. Light Pink   10. Sky Blue   11. Green

Beautiful Cities and Landmarks
Color by Number
Mosaic World Geography
Coloring Book For Adults

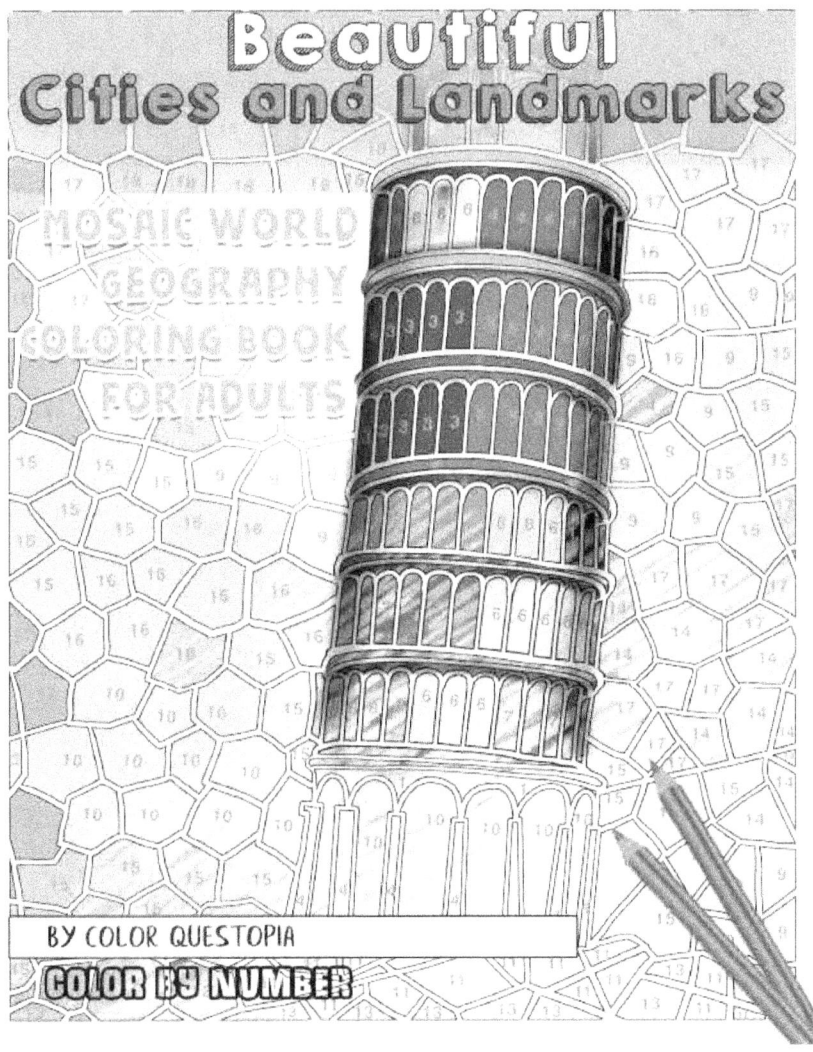

1. Light Brown
2. Medium Brown
3. Dark Brown
4. Gray
5. Dark Gray
6. Yellow
7. Orange
8. Brown
9. Soft Violet
10. Green
11. Deep Green
12. Light Green
13. Medium Gray
14. Light Gray
15. Navy Blue
16. Sky Blue
17. Light Pink
18. Dark Yellow

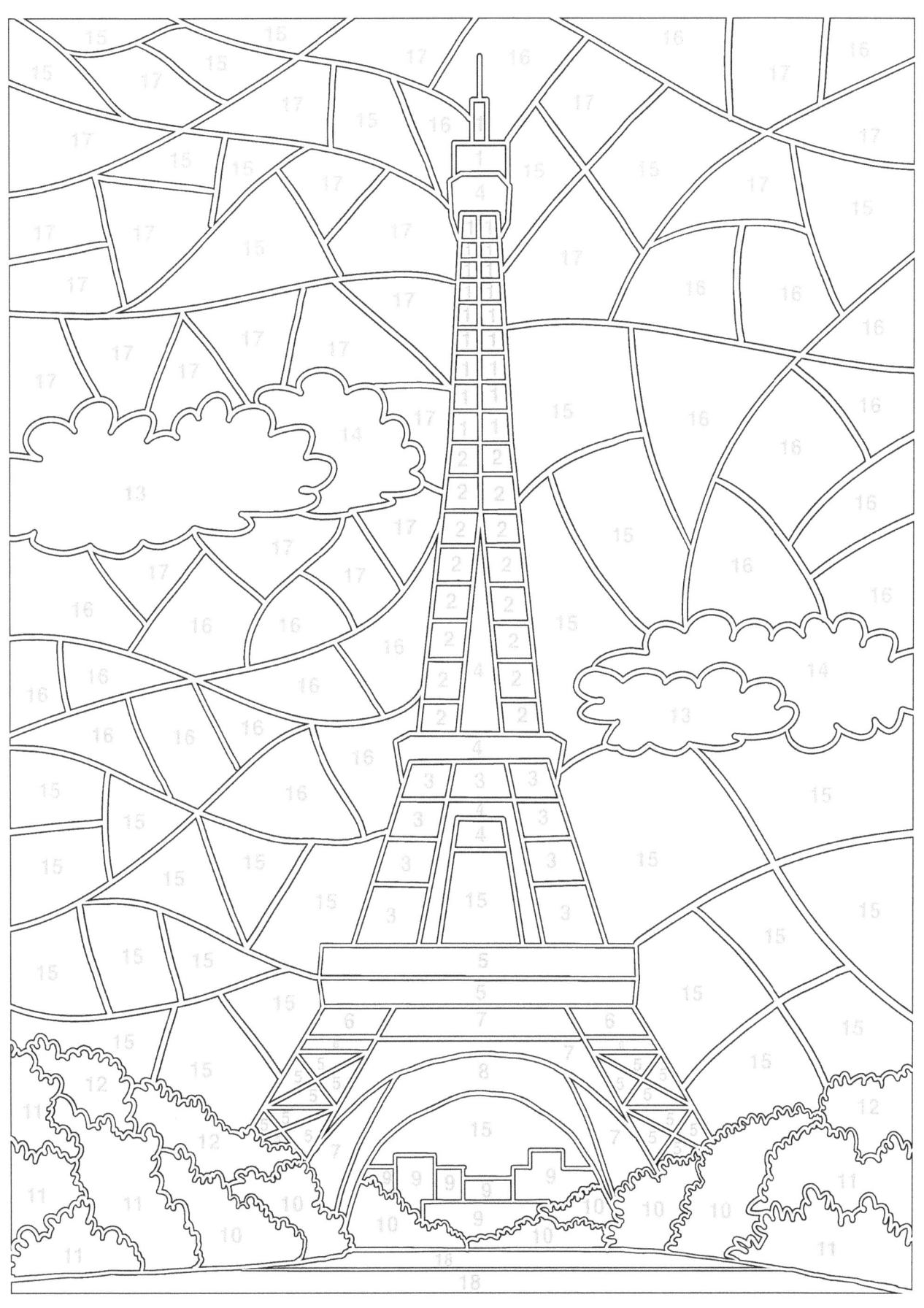

Amazing Owls
Mosaic Color by Number
Adult Coloring Book for Stress Relief
and Relaxation

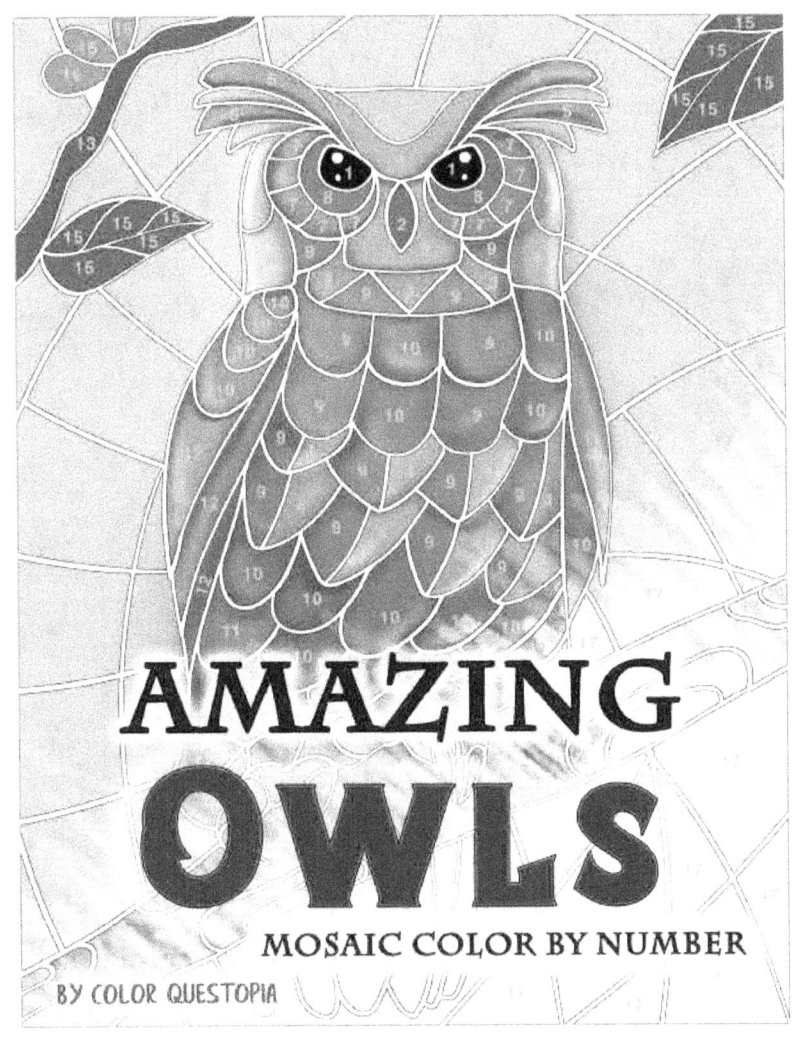

1. Black

2. Light Red

3. Navy Blue

4. Light Violet

5. Dark Orange

6. Medium Brown

7. Light Brown

8. Yellow

9. Light Orange

10. Orange

11. Light Yellow

12. Dark Yellow

13. Medium Orange

14. Dark Brown

15. Brown

16. Medium Blue

17. Blue

18. Sky Blue

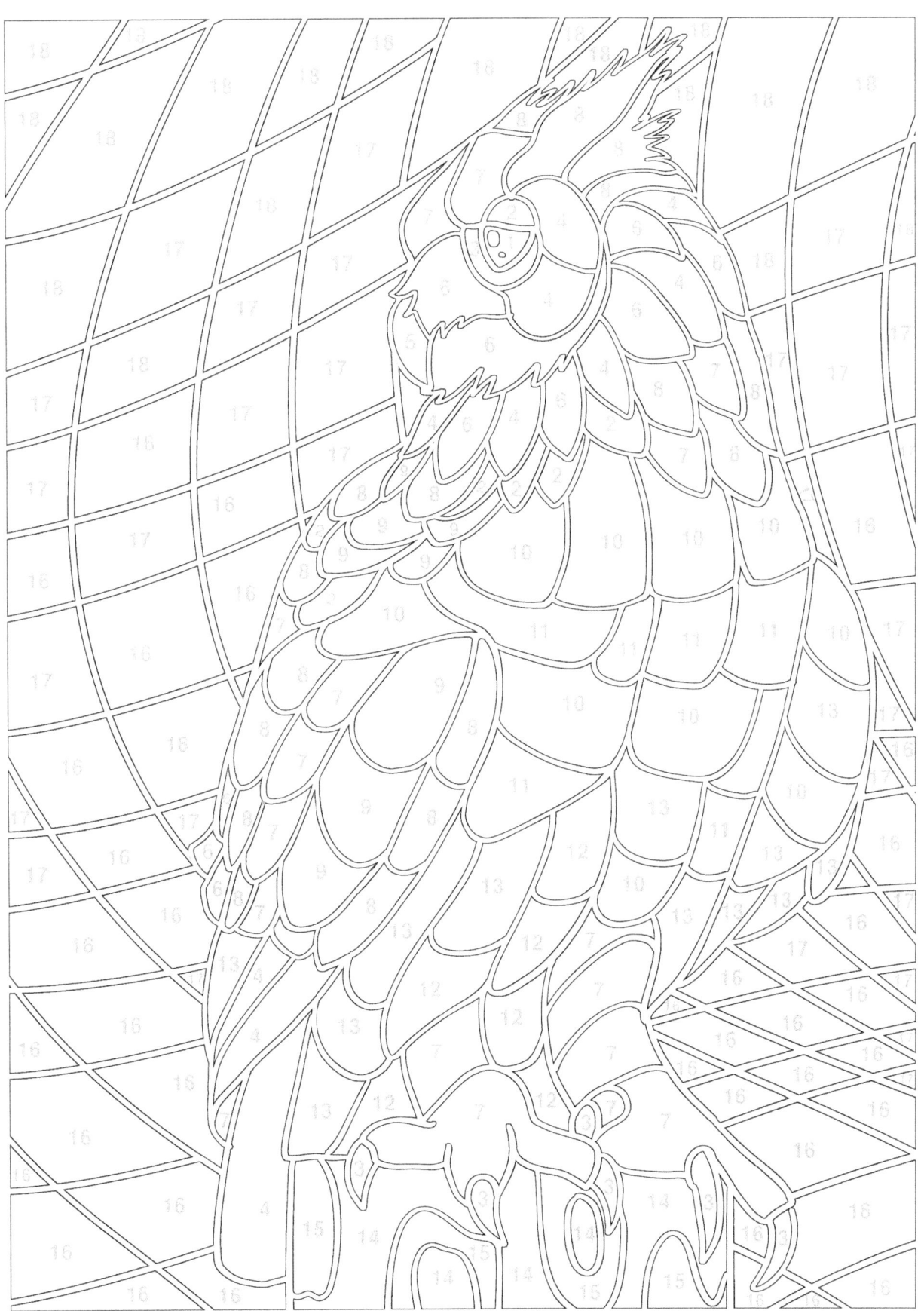

Country Farm Scenes
Nature, Animal, and Easy Designs
Adult Coloring Book
Color By Number For Adults

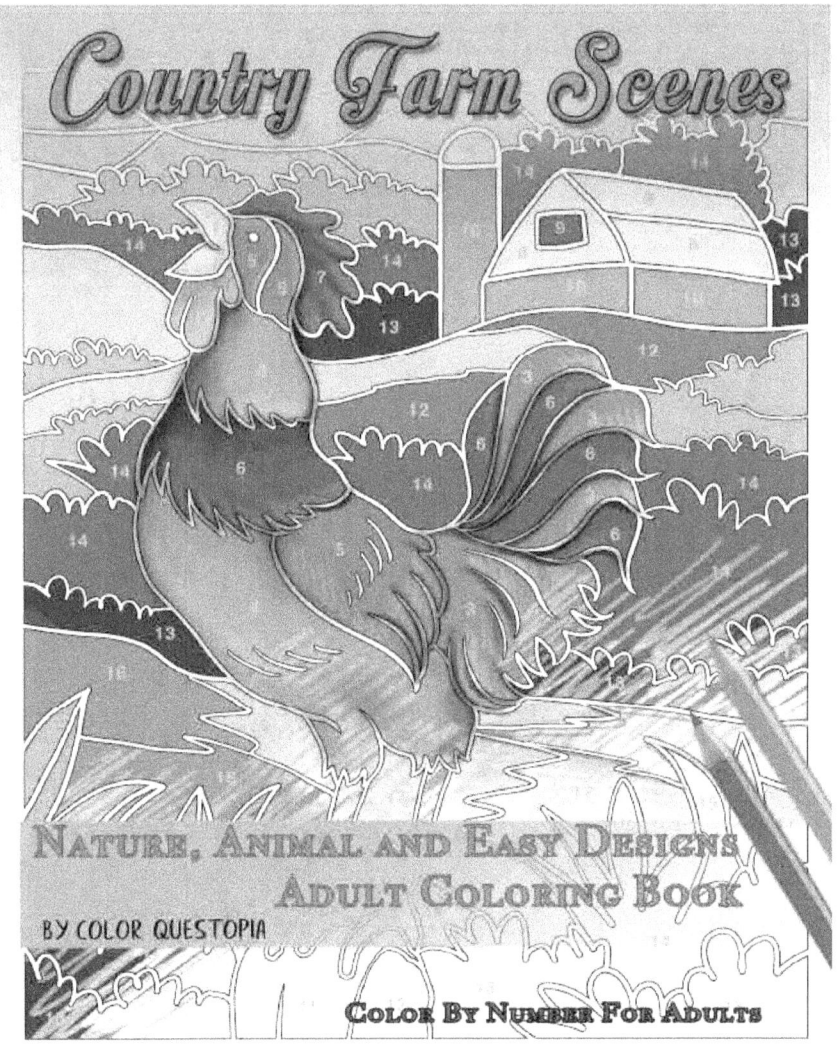

1. Dark Orange
2. Yellow
3. Red
4. Medium Brown
5. Light Gray
6. Orange
7. Dark Green
8. Medium Green
9. Light Brown
10. Brown
11. Light Orange
12. Army Green
13. Light Green
14. Neon Green
15. Dark Brown
16. Gray
17. Light Gray
18. Sky Blue

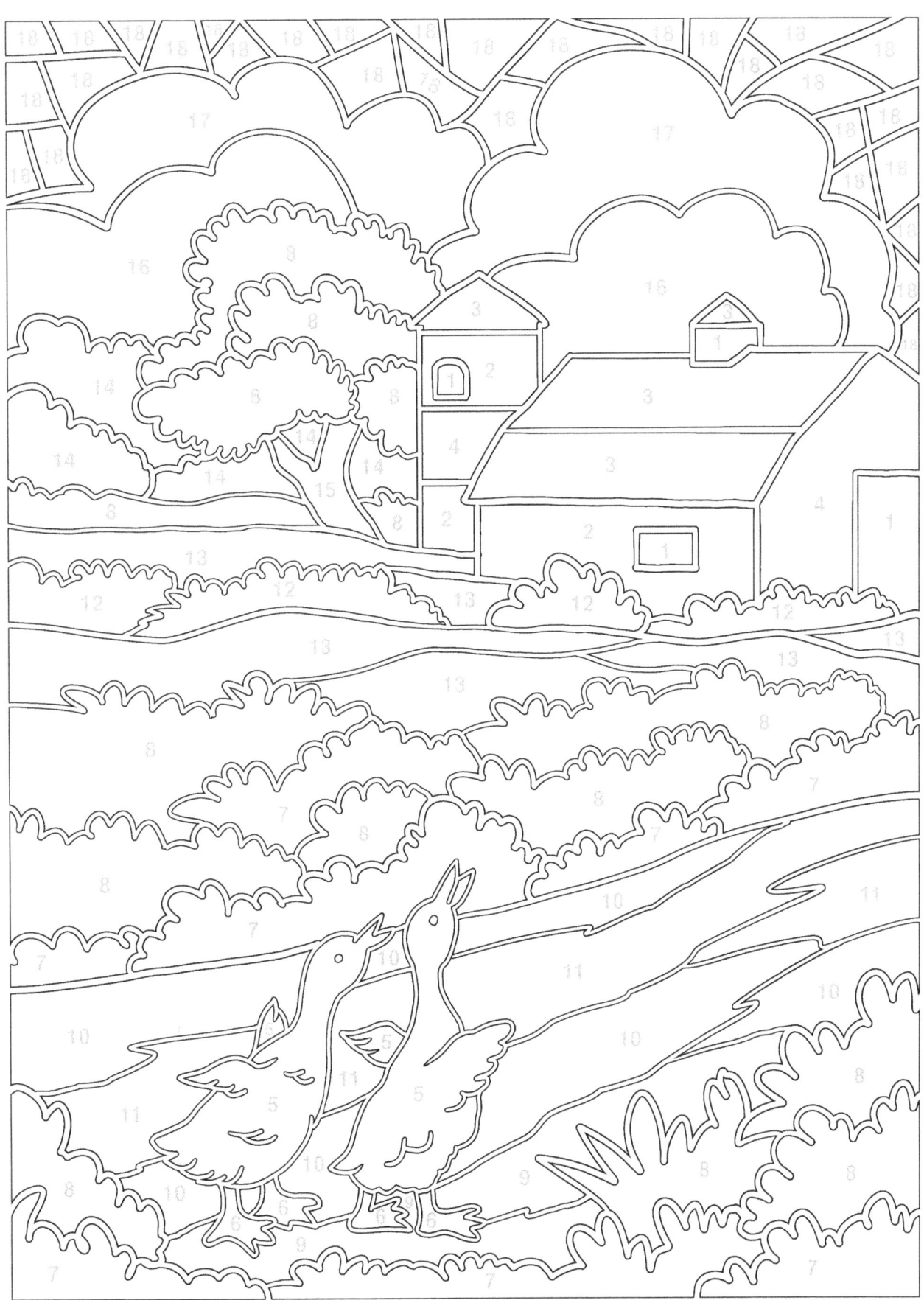

# Horses Jumbo Adult Coloring Book
# Horses and Ponies Grazing and Racing
# Color by Number

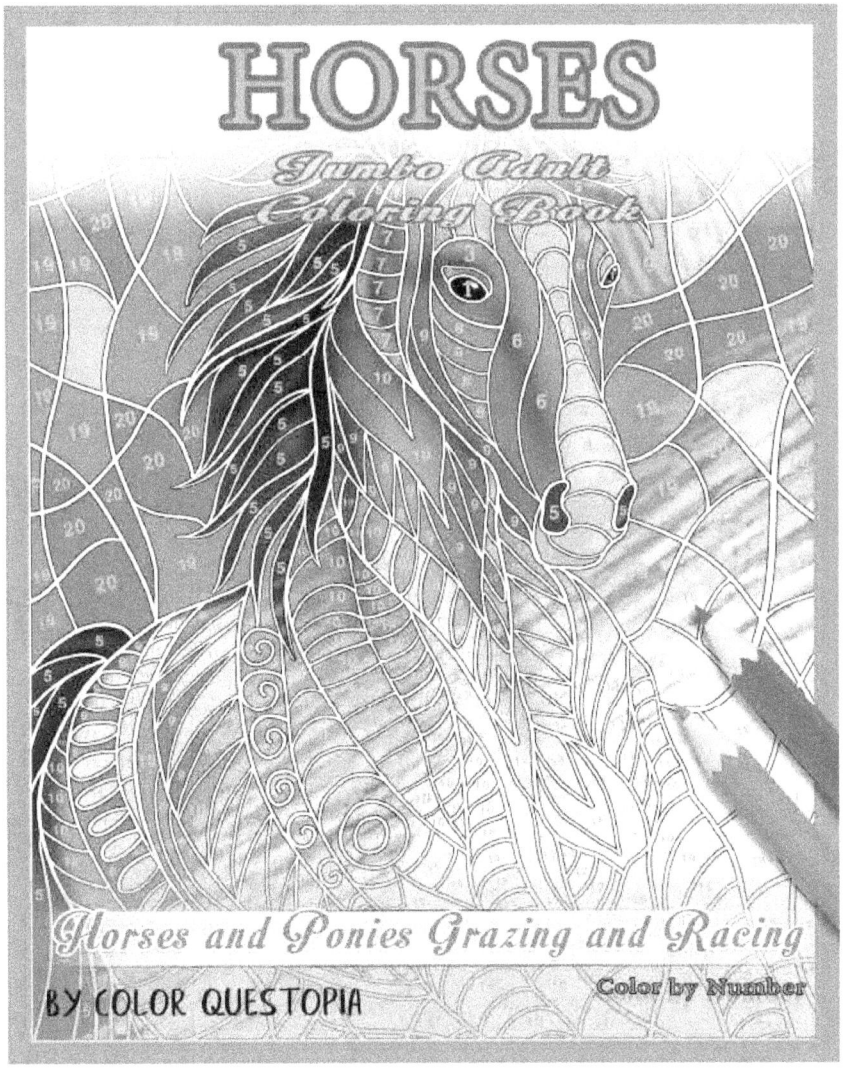

1. Brown
2. Light Brown
3. Dark Brown
4. White
5. Black
6. Light Orange
7. Orange
8. Dark Orange
9. Dark Gray
10. Gray
11. Light Gray
12. Light Green
13. Neon Green
14. Army Green
15. Sky blue
16. Dark Blue
17. Light Blue

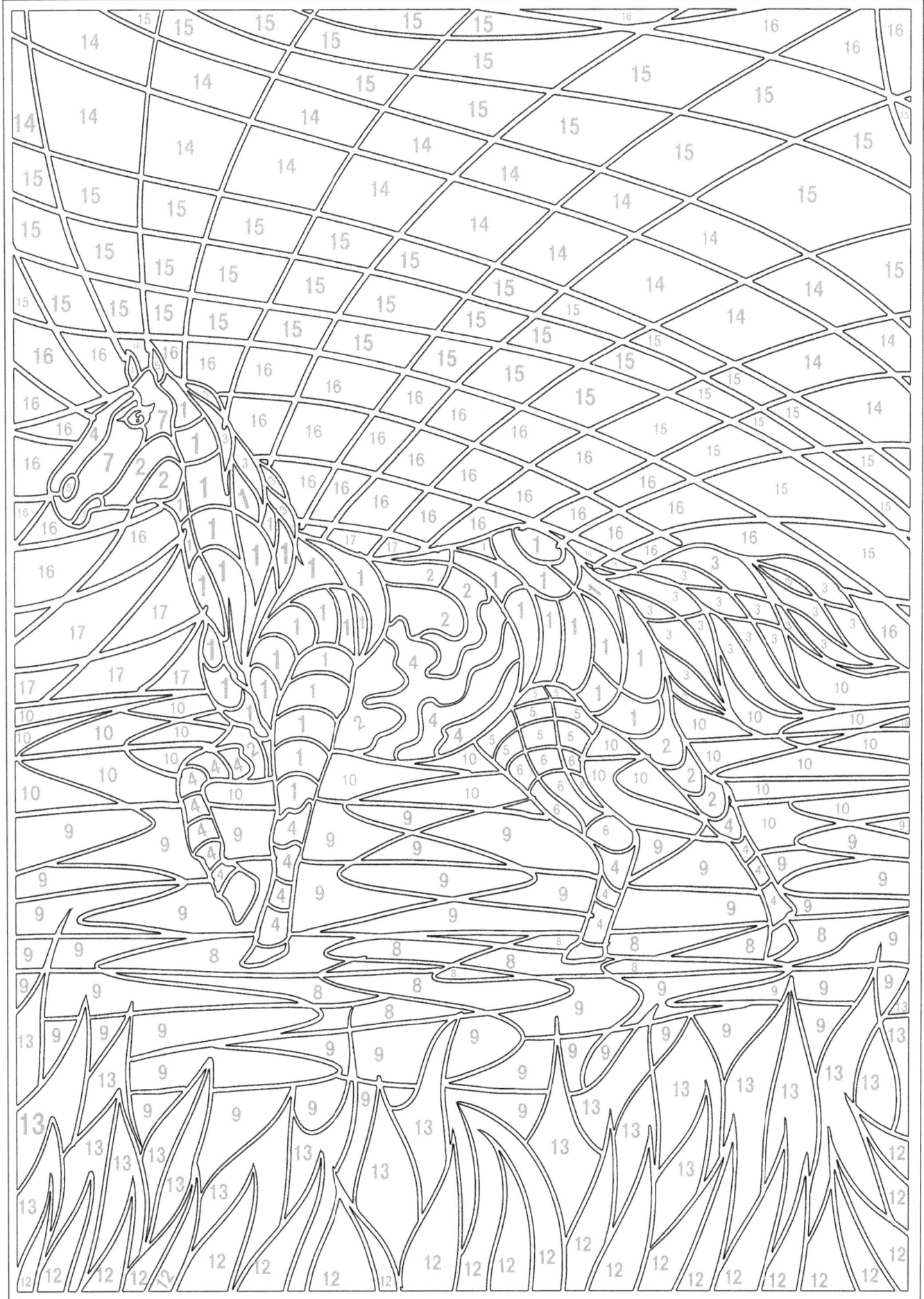

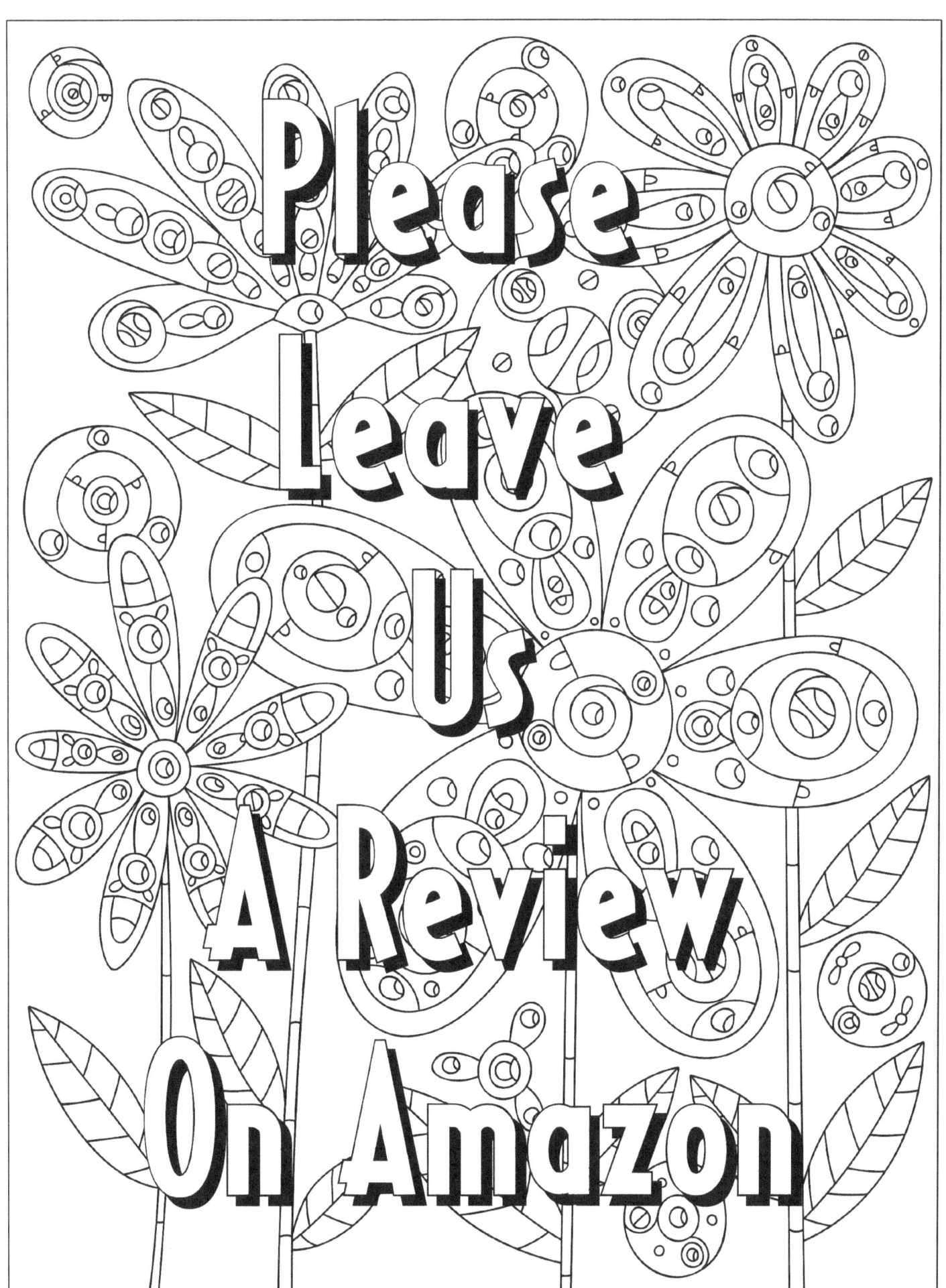